SENIOR ACCOUNTING SERIES

PROCESSING
For Partnerships and Companies

LILIAN VIITAKANGAS
with Alastair Campbell

NELSON
CENGAGE Learning™

Processing for Partnerships and Companies
Senior Accounting Series
4th Edition
Lilian Viitakangas
with Alastair Campbell

Cover design: Brenda Cantell

Any URLs contained in this publication were checked for currency during the production process. Note, however, that the publisher cannot vouch for the ongoing currency of URLs.

First published 2003.
Second (International Standards) edition 2006.
Third edition 2008.
Updated 2010.
© 2003, 2006, 2008, 2010. Xerxes Trust
© 2003, 2006, 2008, 2010. A S Campbell

For product information and technology assistance,
in Australia call 1300 790 853;
in New Zealand call 0508 635 766

For permission to use material from this text
or product, please email **aust.permissions@cengage.com**

National Library of New Zealand Cataloguing-in-Publication Data
Viitakangas, Lilian.
Processing for partnerships and companies/ Lilian Viitakangas with Alastair Campbell. NZ international standards ed.
(Senior accounting series)
Previous ed.: 2003.
Includes index.
ISBN 987-0-17-096280-3
1. Financial statements-New Zealand. 2. Accounting-New Zealand. 3. Accounting-New Zealand-Problems, exercises, etc. I. Campbell, Alastair (Alastair Scott). II. Title. III. Series
657.30993-dc 22

Cengage Learning Australia
Level 7, 80 Dorcas Street
South Melbourne, Victoria Australia 3205

Cengage Learning New Zealand
Unit 4B Rosedale Office Park
331 Rosedale Road, Albany, North Shore 0632, NZ

For learning solutions, visit **cengage.com.au**

Printed in Australia by Ligare Pty Ltd.
2 3 4 5 6 7 14 13 12

CONTENTS

PREFACE

The *Senior Accounting Series* is a range of student workbooks with extensive course notes that has been designed for senior secondary courses and introductory courses at tertiary level. Although it is primarily based on the prescriptions for the National Certificate of Educational Achievement, Levels 3 and 4, the series is suitable for use in other courses where students have already mastered the essential elements of the accounting cycle.

Processing for Partnerships and Companies provides a comprehensive coverage of the accounting process relating to the formation of these entities and the preparation of their year-end financial statements. Additional entries that impact the equity of companies are also included. Full explanations of the accounting process are provided, together with comprehensive examples. Based on the New Zealand Equivalents to International Financial Reporting Standards issued by the New Zealand Institute of Chartered Accountants, this workbook provides detailed summary notes and explanations at a level suitable for students who are developing a deeper understanding of the regulatory framework of accounting and the accounting process.

In addition to the study notes, the workbook provides a variety of tasks, giving students the opportunity to relate the conceptual framework to real world accounting scenarios. The tasks are interspersed with the course notes, resulting in logical flow and content development. Space for completing the tasks is included so that, upon completion of the tasks, the student has a compact summary of notes and applications in a single volume.

2010 Edition

This edition has been completely upgraded in comparison with previous editions. The electronic 2008 international standards edition moved to the New Zealand Equivalent to the IASB *Framework for the Preparation and Presentation of Financial Statements* (issued 2005). This 2010 edition has further updates to reflect changes in the 2007 revision of *NZ IAS 1*, which came into effect for accounting periods beginning on 1 January 2009. Important amendments to the *NZ Preface*, which affect reporting requirements for some companies, have also been included.

Changes to the New Zealand income tax regime, insofar as they affect company tax at this level, have been incorporated. The changes in payment dates for provisional tax have had a considerable impact on the processing of these transactions.

Many of the tasks in the workbook section of the text have been revised and/or replaced. Some new tasks have been designed to reflect the style of NCEA examinations.

ACKNOWLEDGEMENTS

The authors and publishers gratefully acknowledge the invaluable assistance of the following individuals and institutions in the preparation of early drafts of this work:

The students of Diocesan School for Girls, Auckland, Kings College, Auckland, Macleans College, Auckland and St Pauls Collegiate School, Hamilton; Sharon Lofroth of Kings College and Elizabeth Pitu of St Pauls Collegiate for their trialling of the draft manuscript and many helpful comments and suggestions received.

Particular thanks go to Noel Bungay of Macleans College for his painstaking proof-reading of the manuscript.

Thanks are due to my former colleagues in the Department of Accounting and Finance at The University of Auckland: Lloyd Austin, Bruce Bennett and Mike Bradbury for many helpful discussions and technical guidance

The principal author continues to acknowledge the assistance of Graham McEwan, formerly of New House Publishers who patiently, and with great skill, prepared more than thirty volumes for publication over a period of more than 20 years. The co-operation of David Heap and New House Publishers Limited in the production and distribution of many copies of the early trial manuscripts is also gratefully acknowledged.

PARTNERSHIP FORMATION

This chapter is concerned with the accounting entries required to enter partnership transactions into the accounting records. Partnerships have more than one owner and this means that processing their accounting information differs from that of sole traders in some respects. There are two important areas of difference:

- formation of the partnership entity (this chapter)
- distribution of the partnership profit (the following chapter).

How is a partnership formed?

There are three common ways a partnership may be formed:

- Two or more individuals may invest cash and begin a business from scratch.
- A sole trader may decide to take on a partner in return for an investment of cash or other assets in the firm.
- Two existing sole traders may decide to amalgamate their businesses.

1   Two or more individuals invest cash

Example 1

Andrews and Brown agree to set up a partnership on 1 July 2014 to grow and export flowers. Andrews invests $250,000 in cash for a 60% share of profits and Brown invests $200,000 in cash in return for 40% of the profits.

The journal entries to account for the formation of the partnership are shown below.

Andrews and Brown
General Journal   **Page 1**

Date	Particulars	Dr $	Cr $
2014 Jul 1	Bank	250,000	
	Andrews – Capital		250,000
	(for cash invested by Andrews at commencement of partnership)		
	Bank	200,000	
	Brown – Capital		200,000
	(for cash invested by Brown at commencement of partnership)		

> **REMEMBER!**
>
> In a partnership, individual partners have **separate** capital accounts.

NOTE: It would be possible to combine these journal entries into one entry. (In practice, the above entries would appear in the cash receipts journal.) However, when partnerships are being formed it is good practice to prepare separate journal entries for the contribution by each partner, particularly when partners contribute non-cash assets.

The equity accounts in the general ledger appear as follows:

Andrews and Brown
General Ledger

Andrews – Capital   510

Date	Particulars	Ref	Dr $	Cr $	Balance $
2014 Jul 1	Bank	GJ1		250,000	250,000 Cr

Brown – Capital   520

Date	Particulars	Ref	Dr $	Cr $	Balance $
2014 Jul 1	Bank	GJ1		200,000	200,000 Cr

The opening statement of financial position of the partnership is as follows:

Andrews and Brown
Statement of Financial Position as at 1 July 2014

	$
ASSETS	
Current assets	
Bank	450,000
Total assets	**$450,000**
EQUITY	
Andrews – Capital	250,000
Brown – Capital	200,000
Total equity	**$450,000**

Example 2

Carol and Dana agree to set up a partnership as Local Couriers on 1 May 2017. Carol invests a van valued at $15,000. Dana invests a computer system valued at $5,000 and cash of $10,000. Profits are to be shared equally.

The journal entries to account for the formation of the partnership are shown below.

Carol and Dana *trading as*
Local Couriers
General Journal — Page 1

Date	Particulars	Dr $	Cr $
2017 May 1	Van	15,000	
	Carol – Capital		15,000
	(for van invested by Carol at commencement of partnership)		
	Computer system	5,000	
	Bank	10,000	
	Dana – Capital		15,000
	(for computer system and cash invested by Dana at commencement of partnership)		

REMEMBER!

In a partnership, individual partners have **separate** capital accounts.

The equity accounts in the general ledger appear as follows:

Carol and Dana *trading as*
Local Couriers
General Ledger

Carol – Capital — 510

Date	Particulars	Ref	Dr $	Cr $	Balance $
2017 May 1	Van	GJ1		15,000	15,000 Cr

Dana – Capital — 520

Date	Particulars	Ref	Dr $	Cr $	Balance $
2017 May 1	Computer system	GJ1		5,000	5,000 Cr
	Bank	GJ1		10,000	15,000 Cr

The opening statement of financial position of the partnership is as follows:

Carol and Dana *trading as* Local Couriers
Statement of Financial Position as at 1 May 2017

	Note	$
ASSETS		
Non-current assets		
Property, plant and equipment	1	20,000
Current assets		
Bank		10,000
Total assets		**$30,000**
EQUITY		
Carol – Capital		15,000
Dana – Capital		15,000
Total equity		**$30,000**

Notes to the Statement of Financial Position

1 *Property, plant and equipment*	*Cost $*
Van	15,000
Computer system	5,000
	$20,000

NOTE

In a partnership, the individual partners are the legal entities and should be named in the financial statements.

The trading name of the business should also be shown.

2 A sole trader takes a partner in return for investment of cash or other assets

In this situation it is common to review the carrying amounts of the assets and liabilities of the existing firm before admitting the new partner. Since a new accounting entity is formed, the new amounts for assets will represent the historical cost of those assets to the partnership. The carrying amounts of assets in the books of the *old* firm are not relevant to the partnership.

Property, plant and equipment are transferred to the partnership at agreed values. There is no accumulated depreciation in the partnership books because a new accounting entity has been formed. This new entity has no previous history, so no depreciation has accumulated.

Accounts receivable are often revalued. Bad debts are written off in the books of the old firm. Doubtful debts are transferred to the new firm as an allowance for doubtful debts.

Since a partnership is a new entity for GST purposes, it is required to re-register for GST. Thus the common practice is for the owner of the old firm to assume any liability for GST and the partnership will start off with a zero GST balance in the ledger.

When an existing business takes on a new partner, it is usual to start a new set of accounts. Sometimes the old books are used, with the assets and liabilities adjusted to reflect the agreed valuations. In the following example, we will open a new set of accounts.

Example 3

Dora Dainty is in business as a florist. She decided to admit her newly qualified apprentice, Susie Flower, as a full partner to her business as from 1 October 2015. The firm will trade under the name Dainty Flowers. *The trial balance of the business immediately prior to the admission of Susie Flower is shown below.*

NOTE

Property, plant and equipment are transferred to the partnership at their **agreed values**.

There is no accumulated depreciation in the partnership books because it is a new accounting entity.

Dora Dainty
Trial Balance as at 30 September 2015

	Dr $	*Cr $*
Accounts payable		800
Accounts receivable	2,800	
Accumulated depreciation – Equipment		1,200
Accumulated depreciation – Shop fittings		2,400
Accumulated depreciation – Van		12,000
Bank	5,200	
Capital		12,000
Equipment (cost)	2,500	
GST		1,200
Loan – Fantastic Finance (due 2018)		10,000
Shop fittings (cost)	8,000	
Supplies on hand	1,100	
Van (cost)	20,000	
	$39,600	**$39,600**

The partnership agreement specified that:

- *The partnership would take over all of the business assets and liabilities except the bank account, the GST account and the loan. All assets would be recorded at their carrying amounts except for the following revaluations:*

Accounts receivable	*$2,500*
Supplies on hand	*900*
Van	*6,500.*

- *Dora would take over the loan account personally as an advance to the partnership, due for repayment in five years' time.*
- *Susie would introduce sufficient cash to make her capital equal to half of Dora's capital.*

A new set of partnership books is opened, so we begin a new general journal and enter the opening balances at the *cost to the new partnership*.

Dainty and Flower *trading as* Dainty Flowers
General Journal   **Page 1**

Date	Particulars	Dr $	Cr $
2015 Oct 1	Accounts receivable	2,800	
	Supplies on hand	900	
	Equipment	1,300	
	Shop fittings	5,600	
	Van	6,500	
	Allowance for doubtful debts		300
	Accounts payable		800
	Loan – Dainty		10,000
	Dainty – Capital		6,000
	(for sundry assets and liabilities contributed by Dora Dainty at agreed valuations at commencement of partnership)		
	Bank	3,000	
	Flower – Capital		3,000
	(for cash contributed by Flower at commencement of partnership)		

NOTE

The gross amount for accounts receivable is $2,800. However the agreed value is $2,500.

The difference of $300 represents the allowance for doubtful debts.

REMEMBER!

- An *allowance for doubtful debts* has been created to account for the revaluation of accounts receivable.
- There is **no** accumulated depreciation on property, plant and equipment because the partnership is a new accounting entity.

After the journal entries have been posted to the ledger, the partners' capital accounts are:

Dainty and Flower *trading as* Dainty Flowers
General Ledger

Dainty – Capital   510

Date	Particulars	Ref	Dr $	Cr $	Balance $
2015 Oct 1	Sundry assets and liabilities	GJ1		6,000	6,000 Cr

Flower – Capital   520

Date	Particulars	Ref	Dr $	Cr $	Balance $
2015 Oct 1	Bank	GJ1		3,000	3,000 Cr

The opening statement of financial position of the partnership is shown opposite.

Dainty and Flower *trading as* Dainty Flowers
Statement of Financial Position as at 1 October 2015

	Note	$	$
ASSETS			
Non-current assets			
Property, plant and equipment	1		13,400
Current assets			
Bank		3,000	
Accounts receivable	2	2,500	
Supplies on hand		900	
			6,400
Total assets			$19,800
EQUITY AND LIABILITIES			
Non-current liabilities			
Loan – Dainty (due 30 September 2020)		10,000	
Current liabilities			
Accounts payable		800	
Total liabilities			10,800
Equity			
Dainty – Capital		6,000	
Flower – Capital		3,000	
Total equity			9,000
Total equity and liabilities			$19,800

Notes to the Statement of Financial Position

		Cost $
1	*Property, plant and equipment*	
	Equipment	1,300
	Shop fittings	5,600
	Van	6,500
		$13,400

		$
2	*Accounts receivable*	
	Accounts receivable	2,800
	Less: Allowance for doubtful debts	300
		$2,500

3 Two existing businesses amalgamate to form a partnership

Assets and liabilities contributed to the partnership are again recorded at their agreed values.

Example 4

Jean Jones is in business operating as Jean's Jewellery. Jean's friend, Crystal Stone, owns a similar business in a nearby suburb and the two friends have decided to amalgamate their businesses and form a partnership from 1 September 2017. The firm will trade under the name of Crystals and Jewels. Summaries from the statements of financial position immediately before the partnership was formed are shown on the next page.

The partnership agreement specified that:
- *All assets and liabilities of both businesses would be taken over except for the bank and GST accounts.*
- *Jean would pay Vehicle Dealers personally and record a loan at interest of 8% fixed per annum to the partnership for that amount. This loan will be repaid in five years' time.*
- *Carrying amounts would be used for all property, plant and equipment, except for Jean's van which was to be recorded at $12,000.*
- *Bad debts of $1,000 were to be written off for Jean Jones and the remainder of her accounts receivable were to be recorded at $11,100. Crystal Stone's debtors are to be recorded at $5,200.*
- *Crystal was to contribute sufficient cash to make her capital equal to one third of the total capital of the partnership.*

Jean Jones and Crystal Stone
Statement of Financial Position Summaries as at 31 August 2017

	Jones	Stone
	$	$
Bank	5,000	–
Accounts receivable	14,000	6,000
Allowance for doubtful debts	(500)	(200)
Inventory	19,000	3,600
Shop fittings (cost)	6,800	4,800
Accumulated depreciation	(1,700)	(2,400)
Van (cost)	20,000	–
Accumulated depreciation	(5,000)	–
Total assets	**$57,600**	**$11,800**
Bank overdraft	–	1,400
Accounts payable	9,200	2,700
GST	800	500
Loan – Vehicle Dealers (due 31 May 2020)	8,000	–
Capital	39,600	7,200
Total equity and liabilities	**$57,600**	**$11,800**

The journal entries to form the partnership are shown below.

Jones and Stone *trading as* Crystals and Jewels
General Journal   **Page 1**

Date	Particulars	Dr $	Cr $
2017 Sep 1	Accounts receivable	13,000	
	Inventory	19,000	
	Shop fittings	5,100	
	Van	12,000	
	Allowance for doubtful debts		1,900
	Accounts payable		9,200
	Loan – Jones		8,000
	Capital – Jones		30,000
	(for sundry assets and liabilities contributed by Jones at agreed valuations at commencement of partnership)		
	Accounts receivable	6,000	
	Inventory	3,600	
	Shop fittings	2,400	
	Allowance for doubtful debts		800
	Accounts payable		2,700
	Capital – Stone		8,500
	(for sundry assets and liabilities contributed by Stone at agreed valuations at commencement of partnership)		
	Bank	6,500	
	Capital – Stone		6,500
	(for cash contributed by Stone at commencement of partnership)		

The capital accounts of the partners will now appear as follows:

General Ledger
Jones – Capital   510

Date	Particulars	Ref	Dr $	Cr $	Balance $	
2017 Sep 1	Sundry assets and liabilities	GJ1			30,000	Cr

Stone – Capital   510

Date	Particulars	Ref	Dr $	Cr $	Balance $	
2017 Sep 1	Sundry assets and liabilities	GJ1		8,500	8,500	Cr
	Bank	GJ1		6,500	15,000	Cr

The opening statement of financial position for the partnership can now be prepared:

Jones and Stone *trading as* **Crystals and Jewels**
Statement of Financial Position as at 1 September 2017

	Note	$	$
ASSETS			
Non-current assets			
Property, plant and equipment	1		19,500
Current assets			
Bank		6,500	
Accounts receivable	2	16,300	
Inventory		22,600	
			45,400
Total assets			$64,900
EQUITY AND LIABILITIES			
Non-current liabilities			
Loan – Jones	3	8,000	
Current liabilities			
Accounts payable		11,900	
Total liabilities			19,900
Equity			
Capital – Jones		30,000	
Capital – Stone		15,000	
Total equity			45,000
Total equity and liabilities			$64,900

Notes to the Statement of Financial Position

1 Property, plant and equipment	Cost $
Shop fittings	7,500
Van	12,000
	$19,500

2 Accounts receivable	$
Accounts receivable	19,000
Less: Allowance for doubtful debts	2,700
	$16,300

3 *Loan*
The loan from Jones has a fixed rate of interest of 8% and is due for repayment in full on 1 September 2022

KEY POINTS

- A partnership has two or more owners and each owner has a separate **capital** account.

- When new books are opened for a partnership, a separate journal entry is prepared to record the contribution of each partner.

- If the partnership is formed from an existing business, the bank and GST accounts are not normally transferred to the partnership.

- Assets contributed to a partnership are recorded at their **agreed values** to the business.

- **No accumulated depreciation** on property, plant and equipment is transferred to the partnership. (The partnership is a new firm, so has not accumulated any depreciation yet.)

- Any **bad debts** must be written off by the old firm and are not transferred. If there are any doubtful debts included in accounts receivable taken over, an **allowance for doubtful debts** is created for the partnership.

QUESTIONS AND TASKS

1 Mere Stevens and Tama Burns agreed to set up a partnership, *Home-Grown*, to manufacture souvenirs as from 1 October 2019. Each partner has contributed $20,000 in cash. Profits will be shared equally.

a Prepare the journal entries to record the formation of the partnership.

Stevens and Burns *trading as* Home-Grown
General Journal

b Prepare the capital accounts of the partners.

Stevens and Burns *trading as* Home-Grown
General Ledger

Stevens – Capital

Burns – Capital

c Prepare the opening statement of financial position of the firm as at 1 October 2019.

Stevens and Burns *trading as* Home-Grown
Statement of Financial Position as at 1 October 2019

2	Bob Carpenter and Pete Plummer agreed to set up a construction partnership, *Betta Built*, as from 1 November 2015. Bob contributed $10,000 in cash, a truck valued at $20,000 and tools valued at $15,000. Pete contributed a van valued at $15,000, tools valued at $3,000 and plumbing supplies valued at $2,000.

a   Prepare the journal entries to record the formation of the partnership.

Carpenter and Plummer *trading as* **Betta Built**
General Journal

b   Prepare the capital accounts of the partners.

Carpenter and Plummer *trading as* **Betta Built**
General Ledger
Carpenter – Capital

Plummer – Capital

c   Prepare the opening statement of financial position of the firm as at 1 November 2015.

Carpenter and Plummer *trading as* **Betta Built**
Statement of Financial Position as at 1 November 2015

continued

2 c continued   **Carpenter and Plummer *trading as* Betta Built**
Statement of Financial Position (continued) as at 1 November 2015

---

3   Walter Bittle and Bob Large have agreed to set up a partnership business, *Metalworks*, as from 1 June 2017. Bittle contributed $200,000 cash and a van which the partners agreed to have a value of $30,000. Large contributed his premises and equipment, which had agreed values of $175,000 (land $100,000 and buildings $75,000) and $25,000 respectively. Large also contributed sufficient cash to make the capital contributions of the partners equal.

    a   Prepare the journal entries to record the formation of the partnership.

Bittle and Large *trading as* Metalworks
General Journal

    b   Prepare the capital accounts of the partners.

Bittle and Large *trading as* Metalworks
General Ledger

Bittle – Capital

Large – Capital

c Prepare the opening statement of financial position of the firm as at 1 June 2017.

Bittle and Large *trading as* Metalworks
Statement of Financial Position as at 1 June 2017

4 On 1 April 2018, B Friendly and I Render commenced business in partnership trading as *Dateline*. Each partner invested $200,000 cash. On the same day, the firm purchased a computer system for $3,000 cash and bought office furniture on credit for $5,000. Premises were purchased for $250,000 (land $150,000 and buildings $100,000), paying cash of $100,000 as a deposit and raising the balance on mortgage at 8% per annum for 20 years.

a Prepare journal entries in general journal format to record the above transactions. Ignore GST.

Friendly and Render *trading as* Dateline
General Journal

4　a　continued　　　　　　　　**Friendly and Render** *trading as* **Dateline**
General Journal (continued)

b　Prepare the opening statement of financial position of the firm as at 1 April 2018.

Friendly and Render *trading as* **Dateline**
Statement of Financial Position as at 1 April 2018

5　Herbert Longbottom has been in business for three months trading as *Olde Worlde Antiques*. So far the business has been very successful and Herbert has asked his sister Ermyntrude to form a partnership with him, with the object of opening another branch of the firm. They agree that the partnership should commence on 1 July 2016.

continued

5 continued

The firm's statement of financial position immediately prior to the formation of the partnership is summarised as follows:

Herbert Longbottom *trading as* Olde Worlde Antiques
Statement of Financial Position as at 30 June 2016

	Note	$
ASSETS		
Property, plant and equipment	1	40,000
Accounts receivable		6,000
Inventory		150,000
Total assets		$196,000
EQUITY AND LIABILITIES		
Bank		26,000
GST		2,000
Accounts payable		30,000
H Longbottom – Capital		138,000
Total equity and liabilities		$196,000

Notes to the Statement of Financial Position

1 *Property, plant and equipment*	Cost $
Shop fittings	10,000
Van	30,000
	$40,000

The partnership will take over all assets and liabilities at their carrying amounts, except for the GST liability, which Herbert will pay himself. Ermyntrude will introduce sufficient cash to make her capital balance equal to half of Herbert's.

a Prepare journal entries in general journal format to record the formation of the partnership.

Herbert and Ermyntrude Longbottom *trading as* Olde Worlde Antiques
General Journal

b Prepare the capital accounts of the partners.

Herbert and Ermyntrude Longbottom *trading as* Olde Worlde Antiques
General Ledger
Herbert – Capital

Ermyntrude – Capital

5 c Prepare the opening statement of financial position of the firm as at 1 July 2016.

Herbert and Ermyntrude Longbottom *trading as* Olde Worlde Antiques
Statement of Financial Position as at 1 July 2016

6 Albert Oldham is the sole practitioner in a very successful law practice in Hicksville. Due to his impending retirement, he has decided to admit a partner, Ivan Upshot, into the firm as from 1 October 2019.

A summary of the statement of financial position of the firm immediately prior to the formation of the partnership is:

Albert Oldham
Statement of Financial Position as at 30 September 2019

	Note	$
ASSETS		
Property, plant and equipment	1	145,000
Bank		20,000
Accounts receivable		30,000
Total assets		$195,000
EQUITY AND LIABILITIES		
GST		2,500
Mortgage	2	60,000
A Oldham – Capital		132,500
Total equity and liabilities		$195,000

Notes to the Statement of Financial Position

1 Property, plant and equipment	Cost	Accumulated Depreciation	Carrying Amount
	$	$	$
Land	80,000	–	80,000
Buildings	60,000	–	60,000
Office equipment	12,000	10,000	2,000
Office furniture	5,000	2,000	3,000
	$157,000	$12,000	$145,000

2 *Mortgage*

The mortgage is interest-only at a fixed rate of 8% per annum and is due on 30 June 2025.

The partnership agreement specifies the following:
- All assets and liabilities will be taken over except for the bank and GST.
- Assets and liabilities will be taken over at their stated amounts except for the following:
  Land $140,000
  Buildings 110,000
  Accounts receivable 25,000
- Ivan Upshot is to contribute $120,000 cash and immediately after the partnership has been formed, Albert Oldham will withdraw capital of $100,000 in cash.

a Prepare journal entries in general journal format to record the above transactions.

Oldham and Upshot – General Journal

b Prepare the opening statement of financial position for the partnership as at 1 October 2019.

Oldham and Upshot
Statement of Financial Position as at 1 October 2019

7 Trevor Rae and Lily Rose each contributed $300,000 cash to form a partnership on 1 July 2020 for the purpose of purchasing a small publishing business, *Trendy Books*, which is owned by Reid Storey. A summary of the statement of financial position of the firm at the date of acquisition is shown below.

Trendy Books
Statement of Financial Position as at 30 June 2020

	Note	$
ASSETS		
Property, plant and equipment	1	310,000
Bank		25,000
Accounts receivable		120,000
Inventory		170,000
Total assets		**$625,000**
EQUITY AND LIABILITIES		
GST		5,000
Accounts payable		30,000
Mortgage		170,000
R Storey – Capital		420,000
Total equity and liabilities		**$625,000**

Notes to the Statement of Financial Position

1 Property, plant and equipment	Cost	Accumulated Depreciation	Carrying Amount
	$	$	$
Land	150,000	–	150,000
Buildings	100,000	25,000	75,000
Fixtures and fittings	100,000	15,000	85,000
	$350,000	$40,000	$310,000

2 *Mortgage*

The mortgage is interest-only at a fixed rate of 9% per annum and is due on 30 June 2029.

The agreement for sale and purchase contained the following terms and conditions:
- The business would be taken over as a going concern in return for $500,000 cash.
- All assets and liabilities will be taken over except for cash and GST. The amounts shown in the above statement of financial position would be used except that accounts receivable would be taken over at $100,000.

a Prepare journal entries in general journal format to record:

- the formation of the partnership
- the purchase of *Trendy Books*
- settlement with Reid Storey.

Rae and Rose *trading as* **Trendy Books**
General Journal

b Explain the amounts you have recorded in relation to **accounts receivable** in the journal entries you prepared above.

_____

_____

_____

_____

c Explain the amounts you have recorded in relation to **property, plant and equipment** in the journal entries you prepared above.

_____

_____

_____

_____

d Explain why it was necessary to record **goodwill** in the journal entries you prepared above.

_____

_____

_____

_____

e Prepare the **assets** section of the statement of financial position of the firm as at 1 July 2020.

Rae and Rose *trading as* Trendy Books
Statement of Financial Position as at 1 July 2020

ASSETS	Note	$	$

8 Even Stevens owns a bookshop and lotto outlet in a local shopping centre. He has entered into an agreement with Betty Wynn, who owns a local dairy, to form a partnership, *Lucky Break*, as from 1 June. Even will give up the lease on his premises and move his business into Betty's shop.

The journal entry to record Even's contribution to the partnership was as follows:

Stevens and Wynn *trading as* Lucky Break
General Journal

Date	Particulars	Dr $	Cr $
2018	Accounts receivable	1,000	
Jun 1	Inventory	150,000	
	Fixtures and fittings	13,000	
	Allowance for doubtful debts		200
	Accounts payable		18,000
	Capital – Stevens		145,800
	(for assets and liabilities contributed by Stevens at commencement of partnership)		

a In Even's accounts, fixtures and fittings had a carrying amount of $18,000. Suggest **ONE** reason why the fixtures and fittings have not been shown at their carrying amount in this journal entry.

_____

_____

_____

_____

_____

b Explain to Even the purpose of creating an **allowance for doubtful debts** when his contribution to the partnership was recorded.

_____

_____

_____

_____

_____

Betty originally contributed $10,000 of fixtures and fittings and $20,000 of inventory to the business. During June she agreed to contribute a van with an agreed value of $8,000 and sufficient cash to make her capital equal to 25% of the total capital of the partnership.

c **Assuming no other transactions occurred,** prepare Betty's **capital account** in the ledger of the partnership at 30 June 2018.

Stevens and Wynn *trading as* Lucky Break
General Ledger

Wynn – Capital

2018		Dr $	Cr $	Balance $
Jun 1	Sundry assets			30,000 Cr

d Prepare the **assets** section of the statement of financial position of the firm as at 30 June 2018.

Stevens and Wynn *trading as* Lucky Break
Statement of Financial Position as at 30 June 2018

ASSETS	Note	$	$

Notes on the next page

8   continued

Stevens and Wynn *trading as* Lucky Break
Statement of Financial Position as at 30 June 2018

Notes to the Statement of Financial Position

---

9 Herbert Perry owns a small retail outlet which specialises in the sale of motor mowers and chainsaws. Perry Cowen runs a small service and repair shop in premises which he leases at the rear of the shop. The two have decided to amalgamate their businesses and form a partnership trading as *Perry's Mowers* as from 1 April 2017.

The summarised statements of financial position of the respective businesses immediately prior to the formation of the partnership are shown below.

Summary Statements of Financial Position as at 31 March 2017

	Perry	Cowan
	$	$
Bank	20,000	–
Accounts receivable	10,000	5,000
Inventory	30,000	–
Spare parts	–	4,500
Fixtures and fittings (cost)	4,000	–
Accumulated depreciation	(1,500)	–
Tools and equipment (cost)	–	50,000
Accumulated depreciation	–	(10,000)
Land (cost)	105,000	–
Buildings (cost)	45,000	–
Accumulated depreciation	(3,000)	–
Total assets	**$209,500**	**$49,500**
Bank overdraft	–	4,500
Accounts payable	13,000	12,000
GST	1,500	1,000
Mortgage (10%, due 31 May 2025)	70,000	–
Capital	125,000	32,000
Total equity and liabilities	**$209,500**	**$49,500**

The partnership agreement specified the following conditions:
- All assets and liabilities will be taken over except for the bank and GST accounts. The carrying amounts shown in the above statements of financial position would be used except for the following:

	H Perry	P Cowen
Land	$125,000	—
Buildings	70,000	—
Tools and equipment	—	$35,000
Accounts receivable	8,500	4,500

- Perry Cowen will contribute sufficient cash to make his capital equal to that of Herbert Perry.

REMEMBER!

- An allowance for doubtful debts is created to account for the remeasurement of accounts receivable when there is doubt over collection of debtors' accounts.

- There is no accumulated depreciation on property, plant and equipment because the partnership is a new accounting entity.

PHOTOCOPYING PROHIBITED

a Prepare journal entries in general journal format to record the above transactions.

Perry and Cowen *trading as* **Perry's Mowers**
General Journal

Perry and Cowen *trading as* **Perry's Mowers**

continued

9   continued

b   Prepare the opening statement of financial position of the firm as at 1 April 2017.

Perry and Cowen *trading as* Perry's Mowers
Statement of Financial Position as at 1 April 2017

2 ENTRIES TO PREPARE PARTNERSHIP ACCOUNTS

The financial statements that are prepared for a partnership are very similar to those of a sole trader. However, since there is more than one owner, it is necessary to provide some means of allocating the profit between the partners. Thus, as well as the income statement, the statement of financial position and the statement of changes in equity, a **profit distribution statement** (more usually called an appropriation statement) is prepared to achieve this allocation.

Equity Accounts

Earlier, we established that each partner in a partnership has a capital account in the ledger. This is normally used to record only the fixed capital that each partner has agreed to contribute to the partnership. The share of profit attributed to each partner is credited to a second equity account, called the **current** account. Each partner also has a **drawings** account to record withdrawals of cash (or other assets such as goods) from the firm. This drawings account operates in exactly the same way as for a sole trader, and is closed to the partner's current account at the end of the reporting period.

Sometimes a partner may agree to make a loan to the partnership over and above his or her agreed capital contribution. If such a loan is *bona fide* in nature, (in other words, it is a genuine loan to the business) then it is not an equity account, but is a non-current liability in the same way as a loan from any other source. (If the loan is repayable within the next financial year, it will be shown as a current liability.)

Distribution of Profit

The aim of a partnership agreement (in respect of profit-sharing) should be to reward each partner for his or her contribution to the firm. Partners invest capital in the business and many will also work in the firm full-time. Each aspect of the partners' involvement should be recognised by the profit-sharing arrangements. If there is no partnership agreement, the provisions of the Partnership Act 1908 apply and these will often prove inequitable (unfair).

Some typical arrangements for profit-sharing that are found in partnership agreements are:

- partners are credited with interest on the capital they have invested
- partners who work in the firm are credited with salaries
- partners who have advanced loans to the firm are credited with interest on those loans.

Some partnerships also have provisions for interest to be credited on current accounts (or to be charged on overdrawn current accounts). Interest on drawings may also be charged to partners. Sometimes this interest is based on the average drawings throughout the year; other times it may be based on any drawings over and above a certain limit, to discourage partners from withdrawing excessive amounts of cash. The situation varies from firm to firm and it is up to the partners to decide upon the arrangements and record these in the partnership agreement.

Once the division of profits in relation to interest and salaries has been decided, it is necessary to divide the residual profit or loss between the partners according to some arrangement. This may be equally, or on the basis of capital contributions, or by any other formula upon which the partners agree.

The provisions of the Partnership Act 1908 in relation to profit-sharing are as follows:

- no interest is to be paid on capital accounts
- no salaries are to be paid to partners
- no interest is payable on drawings
- interest at the rate of 5% per annum is payable on capital contributions over and above those which have been agreed
- residual profits and losses are to be shared equally between the partners.

The situation relating to interest on current accounts as specified in the Act is unclear. Since the balance of these accounts represents undrawn profits that have been retained in the firm, it can be argued that they represent a contribution over and above that which has been agreed and thus should receive 5% interest.

The arrangements specified in the Act can be very unfair. For example, a silent partner who invests a small amount of capital would be entitled to the same profit share as a working partner who has also made a substantial capital contribution. For this reason, it is very important to have a partnership agreement which specifies a fair profit distribution formula. This formula should reflect:

- reward for effort (ie salary)
- reward for risk (ie interest on capital invested); and
- a means of dividing the residue.

Example

Alpha and Beta are in partnership trading as Alphabet, *with a partnership agreement that specifies the following:*

- *Partners share the profits and losses in the ratio of Alpha 3: Beta 2.*
- *Each partner is to be credited with a salary of $20,000 per annum.*
- *Interest on capital accounts is payable at the rate of 10% per annum based on the opening balance.*
- *Interest of 10% per annum is payable on current account balances based on the opening balance for the year.*
- *Interest of 5% per annum is charged on drawings based on the average balance throughout the year.*
- *Interest is payable on advances at the rate of 15% per annum.*

The balances in the various equity accounts at 1 April 2018 were as follows:

Alpha			**Beta**		
Capital	60,000	Cr	Capital	40,000	Cr
Current	10,000	Cr	Current	5,000	Cr
	$70,000			$45,000	

The profit of the firm (before interest and salaries payable to partners) was $132,000 for the year ended 31 March 2019. During the year Alpha had withdrawn $25,000 in cash and Beta $20,000. Alpha advanced a long term loan of $20,000 to the firm on 1 October 2018.

Before we can prepare the journal entries to record the above, we must calculate the various amounts to be credited to and charged against partners:

Interest on Capital
Alpha:	10% * $60,000	=	$6,000
Beta:	10% * $40,000	=	$4,000

Interest on Current Accounts
Alpha:	10% * $10,000	=	$1,000
Beta:	10% * $5,000	=	$500

Interest on Drawings
Alpha:	½ * (5% * $25,000)	=	$625
Beta:	½ * (5% * $20,000)	=	$500

Interest on Loan
Alpha:	$6/12$ * (15% * $20,000)	=	$1,500

We can now establish the profit for the year that is to be shared among the partners. We know that the profit before interest and salaries payable to partners was $132,000. In a partnership, we normally consider salaries to be a distribution of profit, rather than an expense of the business. This follows from the idea that the entity is separate from the owners. However, the interest on a loan from a partner is treated as an expense because it would have been incurred regardless of the source of the loan.

The journal entry to record the interest expense is as follows:

General Journal

Date	Particulars	Dr $	Cr $
2019 Mar 31	Interest expense	1,500	
	Current – Alpha		1,500
	(for interest on advance from Alpha for 6 months @ 15% per annum)		

The interest is credited to Alpha's current account because we are assuming that it has not been paid during the year.

When closing entries have been prepared, the balance in the income summary account will now be $132,000 – 1,500 = $130,500. For a sole trader, we would close this amount to the owner's capital account in the ledger. However, in the case of a partnership, the profits must be shared between the partners. We thus establish an intermediate step, the **profit distribution account**, which enables the profit-sharing to occur. We can represent this process in the following diagram:

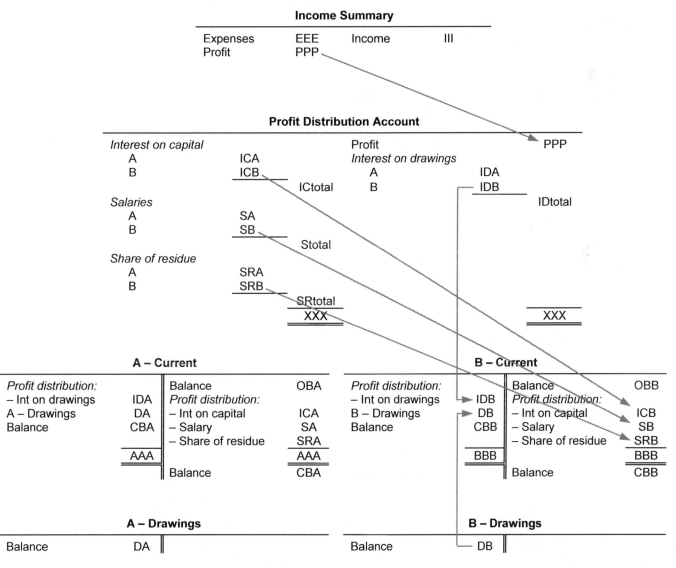

Note: The arrows on the diagram show entries in Partner B's accounts only. Corresponding entries are shown in Partner A's accounts.

When the interest on Alpha's loan has been credited to his current account, the current account in the ledger will appear as follows:

General Ledger

Alpha – Current   511

Date	Particulars	Ref	Dr $	Cr $	Balance $
2018 Apr 1	Balance	b/d			10,000 Cr
2019 Mar 31	**Interest expense**	GJ1		**1,500**	**11,500 Cr**

We are now in a position to distribute the profit between the partners. This takes a number of steps which are outlined below.

Step 1
Close the income summary account to the profit distribution account by transferring the profit. This entry is as follows:

General Journal

Date	Particulars	Dr $	Cr $
2019 Mar 31	Income summary Profit distribution *(closing entry)*	130,500	130,500

The profit distribution account now appears as follows:

General Ledger

Profit Distribution   530

Date	Particulars	Ref	Dr $	Cr $	Balance $
2019 Mar 31	**Income summary**	GJ1		**130,500**	**130,500 Cr**

Step 2
Since we are charging interest on partners' drawings, we credit these to the profit distribution account. The interest is charged against the partners' current accounts. The journal entry is:

General Journal

Date	Particulars	Dr $	Cr $
2019 Mar 31	Alpha – Current Beta – Current Profit distribution *(for interest charged on drawings @ 10% per annum based on average monthly balance)*	625 500	1,125

The profit distribution account and the partners' current accounts now appear as follows:

General Ledger

Profit Distribution   530

Date	Particulars	Ref	Dr $	Cr $	Balance $
2019 Mar 31	Income summary	GJ1		130,500	130,500 Cr
	Interest on drawings:				
	Alpha	GJ1		**625**	**131,125 Cr**
	Beta	GJ1		**500**	**131,625 Cr**

General Ledger

Alpha – Current   511

Date	Particulars	Ref	Dr $	Cr $	Balance $	
2018 Apr 1	Balance	b/d			10,000	Cr
2019 Mar 31	Interest expense	GJ1		1,500	11,500	Cr
	Profit distribution:					
	Interest on drawings	**GJ1**	**625**		**10,875**	**Cr**

REMEMBER!

Interest on drawings is *debited* to the partners' current accounts.

Beta – Current   521

Date	Particulars	Ref	Dr $	Cr $	Balance $	
2018 Apr 1	Balance	b/d			5,000	Cr
2019 Mar 31	**Profit distribution:**					
	Interest on drawings	**GJ1**	**500**		**4,500**	**Cr**

Step 3

The interest on partners' capital accounts is charged against the profit and credited to the individual current accounts. The journal entry is as follows:

General Journal

Date	Particulars	Dr $	Cr $
2019 Mar 31	Profit distribution	10,000	
	Alpha – Current		6,000
	Beta – Current		4,000
	(for interest on capital accounts at 10% per annum)		

The profit distribution account and the partners' current accounts now appear as follows:

General Ledger

Profit Distribution   530

Date	Particulars	Ref	Dr $	Cr $	Balance $	
2019 Mar 31	Income summary	GJ1		130,500	130,500	Cr
	Interest on drawings:					
	Alpha	GJ1		625	131,125	Cr
	Beta	GJ1		500	131,625	Cr
	Interest on capital:					
	Alpha	**GJ1**	**6,000**		**125,625**	**Cr**
	Beta	**GJ1**	**4,000**		**121,625**	**Cr**

Alpha – Current   511

Date	Particulars	Ref	Dr $	Cr $	Balance $	
2018 Apr 1	Balance	b/d			10,000	Cr
2019 Mar 31	Interest expense	GJ1		1,500	11,500	Cr
	Profit distribution:					
	Interest on drawings	GJ1	625		10,875	Cr
	Interest on capital	**GJ1**		**6,000**	**16,875**	**Cr**

REMEMBER!

Interest on capital is *credited* to the partners' current accounts.

General Ledger

Beta – Current   521

Date	Particulars	Ref	Dr $	Cr $	Balance $	
2018 Apr 1	Balance	b/d			5,000	Cr
2019 Mar 31	*Profit distribution:*					
	Interest on drawings	GJ1	500		4,500	Cr
	Interest on capital	**GJ1**		**4,000**	**8,500**	**Cr**

Step 4

The interest on partners' current accounts is charged against the profit and credited to the individual current accounts. The journal entry is as follows:

General Journal

Date	Particulars	Dr $	Cr $
2019 Mar 31	Profit distribution	1,500	
	Alpha – Current		1,000
	Beta – Current		500
	(for interest on current accounts at 10% per annum based on the opening balance)		

The profit distribution account and the partners' current accounts now appear as follows:

General Ledger

Profit Distribution   530

Date	Particulars	Ref	Dr $	Cr $	Balance $	
2019 Mar 31	Income summary	GJ1		130,500	130,500	Cr
	Interest on drawings:					
	Alpha	GJ1		625	131,125	Cr
	Beta	GJ1		500	131,625	Cr
	Interest on capital:					
	Alpha	GJ1	6,000		125,625	Cr
	Beta	GJ1	4,000		121,625	Cr
	Interest on current:					
	Alpha	**GJ1**	**1,000**		**120,625**	**Cr**
	Beta	**GJ1**	**500**		**120,125**	**Cr**

Alpha – Current   511

Date	Particulars	Ref	Dr $	Cr $	Balance $	
2018 Apr 1	Balance	b/d			10,000	Cr
2019 Mar 31	Interest expense	GJ1		1,500	11,500	Cr
	Profit distribution:					
	Interest on drawings	GJ1	625		10,875	Cr
	Interest on capital	GJ1		6,000	16,875	Cr
	Interest on current	**GJ1**		**1,000**	**17,875**	**Cr**

Beta – Current   521

Date	Particulars	Ref	Dr $	Cr $	Balance $	
2018 Apr 1	Balance	b/d			5,000	Cr
2019 Mar 31	*Profit distribution:*					
	Interest on drawings	GJ1	500		4,500	Cr
	Interest on capital	GJ1		4,000	8,500	Cr
	Interest on current	**GJ1**		**500**	**9,000**	**Cr**

> **REMEMBER!**
>
> Interest on current accounts is *credited* to the partners' current accounts unless the current accounts are overdrawn in which case the interest charged (if any) is *debited* to the current accounts.

Step 5

Partners' salaries are now charged against the profit and credited to the individual current accounts. The journal entry is as follows:

General Journal

Date	Particulars	Dr $	Cr $
2019 Mar 31	Profit distribution	40,000	
	Alpha – Current		20,000
	Beta – Current		20,000
	(for salaries payable to partners)		

The profit distribution account and the partners' current accounts now appear as follows:

General Ledger

Profit Distribution   530

Date	Particulars	Ref	Dr $	Cr $	Balance $	
2019 Mar 31	Income summary	GJ1		130,500	130,500	Cr
	Interest on drawings:					
	Alpha	GJ1		625	131,125	Cr
	Beta	GJ1		500	131,625	Cr
	Interest on capital:					
	Alpha	GJ1	6,000		125,625	Cr
	Beta	GJ1	4,000		121,625	Cr
	Interest on current:					
	Alpha	GJ1	1,000		120,625	Cr
	Beta	GJ1	500		120,125	Cr
	Salaries:					
	Alpha	GJ1	**20,000**		**100,125**	**Cr**
	Beta	GJ1	**20,000**		**80,125**	**Cr**

Alpha – Current   511

Date	Particulars	Ref	Dr $	Cr $	Balance $	
2018 Apr 1	Balance	b/d			10,000	Cr
2019 Mar 31	Interest expense	GJ1		1,500	11,500	Cr
	Profit distribution:					
	Interest on drawings	GJ1	625		10,875	Cr
	Interest on capital	GJ1		6,000	16,875	Cr
	Interest on current	GJ1		1,000	17,875	Cr
	Salary	**GJ1**		**20,000**	**37,875**	**Cr**

Beta – Current   521

Date	Particulars	Ref	Dr $	Cr $	Balance $	
2018 Apr 1	Balance	b/d			5,000	Cr
2019 Mar 31	*Profit distribution:*					
	Interest on drawings	GJ1	500		4,500	Cr
	Interest on capital	GJ1		4,000	8,500	Cr
	Interest on current	GJ1		500	9,000	Cr
	Salary	**GJ1**		**20,000**	**29,000**	**Cr**

REMEMBER!

Partners' salaries are *credited* to their current accounts.

Step 6

The final step in allocating the profit is to calculate the residue and share this between the partners. The partnership agreement between Alpha and Beta specifies that the partners are to share profits and losses in the ratio of 60% Alpha to 40% Beta.

The balance in the profit distribution account at this point is $80,125. Alpha's current account will be credited with 60% of this amount (60% x $80,125 = $48,075) and Beta's current account will be credited with the remaining 40% (40% x $80,125 = $32,050). The journal entry is as follows:

General Journal

Date	Particulars	Dr $	Cr $
2019 Mar 31	Profit distribution	80,125	
	Alpha – Current		48,075
	Beta – Current		32,050
	(for share of residue)		

The profit distribution account now appears as follows:

General Ledger

Profit Distribution   530

Date	Particulars	Ref	Dr $	Cr $	Balance $	
2019 Mar 31	Income summary	GJ1		130,500	130,500	Cr
	Interest on drawings:					
	Alpha	GJ1		625	131,125	Cr
	Beta	GJ1		500	131,625	Cr
	Interest on capital:					
	Alpha	GJ1	6,000		125,625	Cr
	Beta	GJ1	4,000		121,625	Cr
	Interest on current:					
	Alpha	GJ1	1,000		120,625	Cr
	Beta	GJ1	500		120,125	Cr
	Salaries:					
	Alpha	GJ1	20,000		100,125	Cr
	Beta	GJ1	20,000		80,125	Cr
	Share of residue:					
	Alpha	**GJ1**	**48,075**		**32,050**	**Cr**
	Beta	**GJ1**	**32,050**		—	

The profit distribution account is now closed because all of the profit has been transferred to the partners' current accounts. The current accounts appear as follows:

General Ledger

Alpha – Current   511

Date	Particulars	Ref	Dr $	Cr $	Balance $	
2018 Apr 1	Balance	b/d			10,000	Cr
2019 Mar 31	Interest expense	GJ1		1,500	11,500	Cr
	Profit distribution:					
	Interest on drawings	GJ1	625		10,875	Cr
	Interest on capital	GJ1		6,000	16,875	Cr
	Interest on current	GJ1		1,000	17,875	Cr
	Salary	GJ1		20,000	37,875	Cr
	Share of residue	**GJ1**		**48,075**	**85,950**	**Cr**

REMEMBER!

The profit distribution account is *closed* to partners' current accounts.

General Ledger

Beta – Current   521

Date	Particulars	Ref	Dr $	Cr $	Balance $	
2018 Apr 1	Balance	b/d			5,000	Cr
2019 Mar 31	*Profit distribution:*					
	Interest on drawings	GJ1	500		4,500	Cr
	Interest on capital	GJ1		4,000	8,500	Cr
	Interest on current	GJ1		500	9,000	Cr
	Salary	GJ1		20,000	29,000	Cr
	Share of residue	**GJ1**		**32,050**	**61,050**	**Cr**

Step 7

The final step is to close the partners' drawings accounts off against their current accounts. This is similar to closing the drawings for a sole trader – the drawings account is a temporary account which must be closed to equity at the end of the reporting period. The journal entries are as follows:

General Journal

Date	Particulars	Dr $	Cr $
2019 Mar 31	Alpha – Current	25,000	
	Alpha – Drawings		25,000
	(closing entry)		
	Beta – Current	20,000	
	Beta – Drawings		20,000
	(closing entry)		

When these entries have been posted, the partners' drawings accounts are closed:

General Ledger

Alpha – Drawings   512

Date	Particulars	Ref	Dr $	Cr $	Balance $	
2019 Mar 31	Balance	b/d			25,000	Dr
	Alpha – Current	**GJ1**	-	**25,000**	—	

Alpha – Current   511

Date	Particulars	Ref	Dr $	Cr $	Balance $	
2018 Apr 1	Balance	b/d			10,000	Cr
2019 Mar 31	Interest expense	GJ1		1,500	11,500	Cr
	Profit distribution:					
	Interest on drawings	GJ1	625		10,875	Cr
	Interest on capital	GJ1		6,000	16,875	Cr
	Interest on current	GJ1		1,000	17,875	Cr
	Salary	GJ1		20,000	37,875	Cr
	Share of residue	GJ1		48,075	85,950	Cr
	Alpha – Drawings	**GJ1**	**25,000**		**60,950**	**Cr**

Beta – Drawings   522

Date	Particulars	Ref	Dr $	Cr $	Balance $	
2019 Mar 31	Balance	b/d			20,000	Dr
	Beta – Current	**GJ1**		**20,000**	—	

REMEMBER!

Partners' drawings accounts are *closed* to the partners' current accounts.

General Ledger

Beta – Current   521

Date	Particulars	Ref	Dr $	Cr $	Balance $	
2018						
Apr 1	Balance	b/d			5,000	Cr
2019						
Mar 31	*Profit distribution:*					
	Interest on drawings	GJ1	500		4,500	Cr
	Interest on capital	GJ1		4,000	8,500	Cr
	Interest on current	GJ1		500	9,000	Cr
	Salary	GJ1		20,000	29,000	Cr
	Share of residue	GJ1		32,050	61,050	Cr
	Beta – Drawings	**GJ1**	**20,000**		**41,050**	**Cr**

The equity section of the statement of financial position at the end of the year will appear as follows:

Alpha and Beta *trading as* Alphabet
Statement of Financial Position as at 31 March 2019

	Note	$	$
Equity	1		
Capital accounts		100,000	
Current accounts		102,000	
Total equity			202,000

Notes to the Statement of Financial Position

1 Equity	Capital	Current	Total equity
	$	$	$
Alpha	60,000	60,950	120,950
Beta	40,000	41,050	81,050
Total	$100,000	$102,000	$202,000

The Statement of Changes in Equity

We can also present a new statement, the statement of changes in equity, for the firm. This statement shows the reasons for the change in equity between the beginning and end of the reporting period.

The statement of changes in equity is presented in a columnar format, showing each component of equity in a separate column, with a final column showing the totals:

Alpha and Beta *trading as* Alphabet
Statement of Changes in Equity for the year ended 31 March 2019

	Capital Alpha $000	Capital Beta $000	Current Alpha $000	Current Beta $000	Total equity $000
Balance at 1 April 2018	60,000	40,000	10,000	5,000	115,000
Changes in equity for 2019					
Capital contributions			1,500		1,500
Drawings			(25,000)	(20,000)	(45,000)
Total comprehensive income for the year			74,450	56,050	130,500
Balance at 31 March 2019	$60,000	$40,000	$60,950	$41,050	$202,000

Note that the closing equity figure in the statement of changes in equity ($202,000) is the same figure as is shown for the total equity in the statement of financial position extract above.

The Profit Distribution Statement

The details from the profit distribution account in the ledger are shown in a vertical financial statement called the **profit distribution statement** (more usually known as an appropriation statement). This is prepared as follows:

Alpha and Beta *trading as* **Alphabet**
Profit Distribution Statement for the year ended 31 March 2019

		$	$
Profit			130,500
Plus:	*Interest on drawings*		
	Alpha	625	
	Beta	500	
			1,125
			131,625
Less:	*Interest on capital*		
	Alpha	6,000	
	Beta	4,000	
			10,000
			121,625
Less:	*Interest on current*		
	Alpha	1,000	
	Beta	500	
			1,500
			120,125
Less:	*Salaries*		
	Alpha	20,000	
	Beta	20,000	
			40,000
			$80,125
Distributed as follows:			
	Alpha	48,075	
	Beta	32,050	
			80,125
			$80,125

KEY POINTS

- All of the profit in a partnership must be distributed between the partners.
- Each partner has a current account in the ledger, as well as capital and drawings accounts.
- A partner's share of the profit is transferred to the current account.
- The profit is distributed to partners through a profit distribution account.
- All amounts paid or payable to partners (except interest on genuine arms-length loans to the firm) are considered to be distributions.
- The profit is distributed according to the arrangements in the partnership agreement. If there is no agreement, the Partnership Act 1908 applies.
- Drawings are closed off to the current account at the end of the period.
- Partnerships have an additional financial statement (the profit distribution statement) to show the distributions to partners.

QUESTIONS AND TASKS

1 Ross Roberts and Percy Pearce formed a partnership on 1 July 2014. Each contributed $100,000 cash and they began business as a superannuation advisory service. Their partnership agreement specified the following:

- Each partner is to receive a salary of $25,000 per annum.
- Interest on capital is to be paid at 12% per annum based on the opening balance.
- Profits and losses are to be shared equally.

The firm was very successful and in the first year of operation a profit of $120,000 was recorded. Ross Roberts made cash drawings of $30,000 and Percy Pearce withdrew $25,000.

a Prepare the profit distribution account for the partnership at the end of its first year of business.

Roberts and Pearce – General Ledger
Profit Distribution

b Show the partners' current accounts as they would appear in the ledger at the end of the first year.

Roberts and Pearce – General Ledger
Roberts – Current

Pearce – Current

c Prepare the statement of changes in equity for the year.

Roberts and Pearce
Statement of Changes in Equity for the year ended 30 June 2015

	Capital Roberts $	Capital Pearce $	Current Roberts $	Current Pearce $	Total equity $
Balance at 1 July 2014	100,000	100,000	—	—	200,000
Changes in equity for 2015					
Drawings					
Total comprehensive income for the year					
Balance at 30 June 2015					

d Prepare the equity section, with **relevant notes**, of the statement of financial position as at 30 June 2015.

Roberts and Pearce
Statement of Financial Position (extract) as at 30 June 2015

	Note	$	$
Equity			
Capital accounts	1		
Current accounts			
Total equity			

Notes to the Statement of Financial Position

1 _Equity_	Capital $	Current $	Total $
Roberts			
Pearce			
Total			

2 Felicity Fixit and Alice Arkwright commenced medical practice in partnership on 1 April 2017. Each contributed $75,000 cash. Their partnership agreement specified the following:

- Each partner is to receive a salary of $50,000 per annum.
- Interest on capital is to be paid at 10% per annum based on the opening balance.
- Interest on drawings is to be charged at 5% per annum based on the average balance throughout the year.
- Profits and losses are to be shared equally.

In the year ended 31 March 2018, the practice reported a profit of $80,000. The partners made cash drawings as follows: Fixit $30,000; Arkwright $40,000. Drawings were made evenly throughout the year.

a Prepare the profit distribution account for the partnership for the year ended 31 March 2018.

Fixit and Arkwright – General Ledger
Profit Distribution

continued

2 a continued

b Show the partners' current accounts as they would appear in the ledger at the end of the first year.

Fixit and Arkwright – General Ledger

Fixit – Current

Arkwright – Current

c Prepare the statement of changes in equity for the year.

Fixit and Arkwright
Statement of Changes in Equity for the year ended 31 March 2018

	Capital Fixit $	Capital Arkwright $	Current Fixit $	Current Arkwright $	Total equity $
Balance at 1 April 2017	75,000	75,000	—	—	150,000
Changes in equity for 2018					
Drawings					
Total comprehensive income for the year					
Balance at 31 March 2018					

d Prepare the equity section, with **relevant notes**, of the statement of financial position as at 31 March 2018.

Fixit and Arkwright
Statement of Financial Position (extract) as at 31 March 2018

	Note	$	$
Equity			
Capital accounts	1		
Current accounts			
Total equity			

Notes to the Statement of Financial Position

1	Equity	Capital $	Current $	Total $
	Fixit			
	Arkwright			
	Total			

3 Boris Brainz and Boris Bighead are in business as private tutors trading as *Help*, a firm specialising in coaching clinics for accounting students who are in danger of failing their examinations. The following statement of financial position was prepared for the business as at 31 December 2019:

Brainz and Bighead *trading as* Help
Statement of Financial Position as at 31 December 2019

	Note	$	$
ASSETS			
Non-current assets			
Property, plant and equipment	1	8,400	
Reference books		2,500	
			10,900
Current assets			
Accounts receivable			2,300
Total assets			$13,200
EQUITY AND LIABILITIES			
Non-current liabilities			
Loan – Brainz	2		2,000
Current liabilities			
Bank		1,200	
GST		200	
Accounts payable		300	
Total current liabilities			1,700
Total liabilities			3,700
Equity	3		
Capital accounts		9,000	
Current accounts		500	
Total equity			9,500
Total equity and liabilities			$13,200

Notes to the Statement of Financial Position

1 Property, plant and equipment

	Cost	Accumulated Depreciation	Carrying Amount
	$	$	$
Computers	8,000	1,600	6,400
Furniture	2,200	200	2,000
	$10,200	$1,800	$8,400

2 *Loan from Brainz*
The loan from Brainz is interest-only at a fixed rate of 7.5% per annum and is due for repayment in 2023.

3 *Equity*

	Capital	Current	Total equity
	$	$	$
Brainz	4,000	1,500	5,500
Bighead	5,000	(1,000)	4,000
	$9,000	$500	$9,500

The partnership agreement contained the following provisions:

- Each partner is to receive a salary of $10,000 per annum.
- Interest on the loan from Brainz is to be considered an expense of the business.
- Interest on current accounts is to be paid at 6% per annum, based on opening balances. However, if the current account was overdrawn interest is to be charged at 7.5% per annum.
- Interest on capital accounts is to be paid at 5% per annum, based on the opening balances.
- Profits and losses are to be shared equally.

The profit before interest on Brainz' loan for the year ended 31 December 2020 was $22,115. Brainz withdrew $15,000 and Bighead withdrew $10,000 during the year.

3 continued

a Prepare the profit distribution account for the partnership for the year ended 31 December 2020.

Brainz and Bighead *trading as* Help
General Ledger
Profit Distribution

b Show the partners' current accounts as they would appear in the ledger at the end of the year.

Brainz and Bighead *trading as* Help
General Ledger
Brainz – Current

Bighead – Current

c   Prepare the statement of changes in equity for the year.

Brainz and Bighead *trading as* **Help**
Statement of Changes in Equity for the year ended 31 December 2020

	Capital Brainz $	Capital Bighead $	Current Brainz $	Current Bighead $	Total equity $
Balance at 1 January 2020	4,000	5,000	1,500	(1,000)	9,500
Changes in equity for 2020					
Capital contributions					
Drawings					
Total comprehensive income for the year					
Balance at 31 December 2020					

d   Prepare the equity section of the statement of financial position as at 31 December 2020.

Brainz and Bighead *trading as* **Help**
Statement of Financial Position (extract) as at 31 December 2020

	Note	$	$
Equity			
Capital accounts	1		
Current accounts			
Total equity			

Notes to the Statement of Financial Position

1 *Equity*	Capital $	Current $	Total $
Brainz			
Bighead			
Total			

---

4   *BB Bottoms* is a band in the entertainment industry which operates under a partnership agreement. The band tours the country, performing in out-of-the-way hotels and dance halls. The partners, Basil, Bert and Bebe Babble, each contributed $2,000 cash when the partnership was formed on 1 April 2016. In additional, Basil contributed his drum kit which he had just bought for $2,000 and Bebe invested her new guitar which had cost $1,000. Bert agreed to sell his van to the band for $2,500 and this amount was recorded as a loan to the business. Bert has agreed that the interest on his loan be credited to his current account at the end of each year.

The partnership agreement contained the following clauses:

- Each partner is to receive interest on capital at 5% per annum.
- Interest on Bert's loan was to be at 10% per annum. The loan is to be paid back in equal instalments on 31 March for the next five years.
- Residual profits and losses are to be shared in the ratio of capital contributions.

In the year to 31 March 2017, the band accounts showed a profit of $5,200 before interest. Each partner withdrew $1,000 cash during the year. The profit was all in cash because there were no credit transactions and no further non-current assets had been purchased. Depreciation on property, plant and equipment was not considered material, so was not charged.

a   Prepare the journal entries in general journal format to record the formation of the partnership.

Basil, Bert and Bebe Babble *trading as* **BB Bottoms**
General Journal

4 a continued

Basil, Bert and Bebe Babble *trading as* BB Bottoms
General Journal (continued)

b Prepare the profit distribution account for the year ended 31 March 2017.

Basil, Bert and Bebe Babble *trading as* BB Bottoms
General Ledger
Profit Distribution

c Prepare the partner's capital and current accounts and Bert's loan account for the year.

Basil, Bert and Bebe Babble *trading as* BB Bottoms
General Ledger
Basil – Capital

Bert – Capital

Bebe – Capital

Basil – Current

Bert – Current

Bebe – Current

Bert – Loan

d Prepare the statement of changes in equity for the year.

Basil, Bert and Bebe Babble *trading as* **BB Bottoms**
Statement of Changes in Equity for the year ended 31 March 2017

	Capital Basil $	Capital Bert $	Capital Bebe $	Current Basil $	Current Bert $	Current Bebe $	Total equity $
Balance at 1 April 2016							
Changes in equity for 2017							
Capital contributions							
Drawings							
Total comprehensive income for the year							
Balance at 31 March 2017							

4 continued

e Prepare the **equity and liabilities** section of the statement of financial position as at 31 March 2017. Include relevant notes.

Basil, Bert and Bebe Babble *trading as* BB Bottoms
Statement of Financial Position (extract) as at 31 March 2017

EQUITY AND LIABILITIES	$	$

5 Anderson and Williams are in partnership as advisers to prospective real estate purchasers. The following current accounts appeared in the ledger at 31 March 2018:

Anderson – Current

Date	Particulars	Dr $	Cr $	Balance $	
2018	Balance			3,000	Cr
Mar 31	Profit distribution				
	– Salary		25,000	28,000	Cr
	– Interest on capital		3,000	31,000	Cr
	– Share of residue		14,000	45,000	Cr
	– Interest on drawings	500		44,500	Cr
	Anderson – Drawings	25,000		19,500	Cr

Williams – Current

Date	Particulars	Dr $	Cr $	Balance $	
2018	Balance			1,500	Dr
Mar 31	Interest expense		1,000	500	Dr
	Profit distribution				
	– Salary		20,000	19,500	Cr
	– Interest on capital		4,000	23,500	Cr
	– Share of residue		21,000	44,500	Cr
	– Interest on drawings	400		44,100	Cr
	Williams – Drawings	20,000		24,100	Cr

Prepare the profit distribution account for the year and hence calculate the profit of the partnership.

Anderson and Williams
General Ledger
Profit Distribution

ANSWER: Profit = $ _____

---

6 PART A

R Bowling and D Ruggles, trading as *Jobs for the Boys* are in partnership as personnel consultants who specialise in the placement of ex-Members of Parliament in new careers. When the partnership was formed on 1 January 2015 they were confident that it would be a great success and did not feel the need to draw up a partnership agreement.

Bowling's contribution to the partnership was $40,000 in cash. Ruggles contributed $90,000, $20,000 of which was fixed capital with the remainder being a loan to the firm, repayable in full in five years' time. A loan agreement to this effect was drawn up. Interest is payable at 5% per annum on the loan and is to be credited to Ruggles' current account at the end of each year.

Unfortunately, the partner's early optimism was quickly dampened as in the year to 31 December 2015 a net loss of $50,000 was reported before any interest or salaries payable to partners. As a result neither partner was able to take any drawings from the business.

a Prepare the profit distribution account for the year ended 31 December 2015.

R Bowling and D Ruggles *trading as* Jobs for the Boys
General Ledger
Profit Distribution

PART A   continued

b   Show the partners' current accounts as they would appear in the ledger as at 31 December 2015.

R Bowling and D Ruggles *trading as* Jobs for the Boys
General Ledger
Bowling – Current

Ruggles – Current

c   Prepare the equity section of the statement of financial position as at 31 December 2015.

R Bowling and D Ruggles *trading as* Jobs for the Boys
Statement of Financial Position (extract) as at 31 December 2015

d   i   List the factors that would be taken into account when deciding on a suitable profit-sharing arrangement for the partnership.

_____

_____

_____

_____

_____

_____

_____

_____

_____

6 d ii Identify any further information you would require before you could make a recommendation to Bowling and Ruggles concerning a fair profit-sharing arrangement for the partnership.

_____

_____

_____

_____

6 PART B

After further discussions with the partners, it was decided that a fair arrangement would be that interest of 10% per annum would be payable on partners' capital accounts, based on the average monthly balance. No interest would be paid on current accounts unless they were overdrawn at the end of the previous year in which case 10% of the opening balance would be charged. Salaries of $25,000 would be payable to the partners and the interest on Ruggles' loan would be increased to 10% per annum. Residual profits and losses are to be shared in the ratio of year-end contributed capitals. These details were recorded in a partnership agreement.

Fortunately there was a general election the following year and the business flourished, recording a profit of $250,000 before interest and salaries. On 1 July, the partners decided to increase their fixed capital. Bowling transferred his car, which had recently been valued at $30,000 to the business, while Ruggles decided to transfer $15,000 of his loan account to fixed capital. Each partner withdrew $50,000 cash during the year.

e Prepare the journal entries to record the changes to the partners' fixed capital accounts on 1 July 2016.

R Bowling and D Ruggles *trading as* Jobs for the Boys
General Journal

f Prepare the profit distribution account for the year ended 31 December 2016.

R Bowling and D Ruggles *trading as* Jobs for the Boys
General Ledger

Profit Distribution

g   Show the partners' current accounts as they would appear in the ledger as at 31 December 2016.

General Ledger

Bowling – Current

Ruggles – Current

h   Prepare the statement of changes in equity for the year ended 31 December 2016.

R Bowling and D Ruggles *trading as* **Jobs for the Boys**
Statement of Changes in Equity for the year ended 31 December 2016

	Capital Bowling $	Capital Ruggles $	Current Bowling $	Current Ruggles $	Total equity $
Balance at 1 January 2016					
Changes in equity for 2016					
Capital contributions					
Drawings					
Total comprehensive income for the year					
Balance at 31 December 2016					

i Prepare the equity section, including relevant notes, of the statement of financial position as at 31 December 2016.

R Bowling and D Ruggles *trading as* **Jobs for the Boys**
Statement of Financial Position (extract) as at 31 December 2016

---

7 Dave and Dawn are in partnership trading as *Betta Fence*, building fences in a remote country area. Their partnership agreement specifies the following:

- Salaries for Dave and Dawn are $30,000 and $10,000 per annum respectively.
- Interest on capital accounts is paid at 5% per annum, based on the average balance during the year.
- No interest is payable on current accounts, but interest on drawings of more than 10% in excess of the annual salary is charged at 12% per annum from the date that the 10% limit is exceeded.
- Profits and losses are shared in the ratio Dave 3: Dawn 2.

The following balances have been extracted from the ledger at 1 April 2020:

	Capital $	Current $	Loan $	Drawings $
Dave	6,000 Cr	15,000 Cr	—	32,000 Dr
Dawn	20,000 Cr	5,000 Dr	12,000 Cr	12,000 Dr

During the year to 31 March 2021, the following events occurred:

- Drawings were taken evenly throughout the year.
- The partnership repaid $2,000 of the loan from Dawn on 1 October 2020. There had been no interest charged on this loan in the past, but the partners agreed that 12% per annum was payable from the date of this repayment.
- Dave agreed to transfer $3,000 from his current account to fixed capital on 1 August 2020.
- The residue after all other distributions of profit for the year was a loss of $18,000.

a Complete the journal entries shown below in accordance with the descriptions given in the narrations.

Dave and Dawn *trading as* **Betta Fences**
General Journal

2020			
	(for transfer from current to capital by Dave)		
	(for interest on Dawn's loan to the firm)		
	(for interest charged on Dawn's drawings)		

7 **continued**

b Explain the **purpose** of the following journal entry:

Dave and Dawn *trading as* **Betta Fences**
General Journal

Date	Particulars	Dr $	Cr $
2021	Income summary	90,000	
Mar 31	Profit distribution		90,000

_____

_____

_____

c Show **Dave's current account** as it would appear in the ledger as at 31 March 2021.

General Ledger
Dave – Current

d Explain why the **interest on Dawn's loan** is an expense of the business rather than a distribution of profit.

_____

_____

_____

_____

Dawn is thinking of retiring and moving to the city. She is not keen to remain in the partnership once she leaves the area and has asked Dave to buy her share of the business. However, Dave does not have sufficient funds to do so. Dave's friend Ross has expressed an interest but wants a 60% share of the profit. Dave thinks this is too much since Ross is not particularly experienced at building fences and doesn't work very hard.

e Suggest **ONE** reason why Dawn may not be keen to remain as a partner once she leaves the area.

_____

_____

_____

f Make a suggestion as to how Dave and Ross could form a partnership with arrangements that suit both their requirements

_____

_____

_____

_____

3 COMPANY FORMATION

In *The Conceptual Framework* booklet of this series, the company form of business organisation was introduced. The major difference between a company and a sole trader or partnership firm is that the company is a **separate legal entity** from its owners (shareholders). The process of forming a company is called **incorporation**.

The summary below shows the major characteristics of companies.

SOME FACTS ABOUT COMPANIES

- A company is a separate legal entity registered under the Companies Act 1993.
- The capital of a company is divided into units called *shares*.
- The owners of the company are called *shareholders*. A company may have any number of shareholders – a single person can form a company and own all the shares.
- A company is normally run by a *board of directors* on behalf of the shareholders.
- A company and its shareholders are separate *legal* entities as well as being separate *accounting* entities.
- The shareholders of a company have limited liability. This means that if the company becomes insolvent (cannot pay its debts), the shareholders are not personally liable for the debts of the business. All that the shareholders can be required to pay is any amount still owing on their shares. In some circumstances the directors can be held liable for company debts.
- The board of directors is elected by the shareholders.
- The company has an unlimited life. If shareholders die or sell their shares, the company keeps going.
- A *dividend* is a payment to the shareholders of a company that does not involve the repurchase of shares.
- The rules for running the company are laid down in the company's *constitution*. If a company does not have a constitution, the provisions of the Companies Act 1993 apply.

The differences between companies and other types of entities give rise to a number of new accounting transactions that must be recorded for a company. These are:

- issue of shares
- payment of expenses for setting up the company (sometimes called *preliminary expenses*)
- payments to directors
- payment of audit fees
- payment of and provision for income tax
- issue of debentures and payment of interest on debentures
- repurchase of shares
- declaration of and payment of dividends.

Issue of Shares for Cash

To raise its initial capital, or to raise additional capital, a company may wish to sell shares to the public. There is no limit on the number of shares that can be issued, subject to the provisions of the company's constitution. If permitted by the constitution, a company may also issue different types of shares. In this course, we will consider only *ordinary* shares which are the most common. Ordinary shareholders bear the ultimate risk of owning the company – whilst they have limited liability, they stand to lose their entire investment if the company is wound up.

Issues of shares to the public are governed by the *Securities Act 1978*. The company is required to issue a **prospectus**, which must be audited. The prospectus contains details of the company's plans for the future including budgeted financial statements. It also contains an application form for shares.

The Securities Act 1978 (amended 2004) requires that subscriptions (application money) for shares are held in trust until such time as the shares are issued or the money is returned to the applicant. The prospective shareholder completes the application form and sends this, together with the amount payable, to the company's trustee, which is often a sharebroker. Most companies require the full amount payable for the shares to be sent with the application.

The trustee is thus required to hold the money on trust until the shares have been issued (allotted) to shareholders. Once allotment has occurred, the money can be transferred to the company's bank account.

Example 1

Bovine Limited was incorporated on 1 September 2015. On 15 September a prospectus was issued inviting the public to apply for 500,000 shares at a price of $1.00 each, payable in full on application. Applications closed on 20 October, by which time the issue was fully subscribed. Shares were allotted on 31 October.

A summary of the events that occurred and the recording process is shown below.

Event	Recording
Sep 1 Issue prospectus	■ No journal entry required
Oct 20 Applications closed	■ No journal entry required
Oct 31 Shares allotted	■ Record share capital ■ Cash transferred to company bank account by trustee.

Note
- There is no journal entry required to record the issue of the prospectus because no transaction has occurred.
- All application money is paid to the trustee, so no journal entry occurs in the company records.
- When the shares have been allotted the cash is transferred to the company and a journal entry is made in the company's accounts.

The journal entry to record the share issue is shown below. (Note: We will use general journal format throughout this text, although bank entries would normally be recorded in a cash receipts journal.)

Bovine Limited
General Journal

Date	Particulars	Dr $	Cr $
2015 Oct 31	Bank Share capital *(for the issue of 500,000 shares at a price of $1.00 each as per resolution of directors, minute book folio....)*[1]	500,000	500,000

The above example shows the full amount of the proceeds of the issue being paid to the company. In practice, this is extremely unlikely because the trustee will charge the company for processing the share issue. These charges are commonly called **brokerage**.

Brokerage is usually charged at a percentage of the value of the shares sold and is deducted from the proceeds of the share issue. These costs are deducted directly from equity and only the net amount is recorded.

---

[1]   Shares can only be issued by a resolution of the company directors. All resolutions are recorded in the company minute book. Folio refers to the page number of the minute book.

PHOTOCOPYING PROHIBITED

Suppose the brokerage on the above share issue is 2.5%. Brokerage charges are 2.5% * $500,000 = $12,500, leaving $500,000 – 12,500 = $487,500 payable to the company. The journal entry to record the issue of shares becomes:

Bovine Limited
General Journal

Date	Particulars	Dr $	Cr $
2015 Oct 31	Bank	487,500	
	Share capital		487,500
	(for the issue of 500,000 shares at a price of $1.00 each less brokerage of 2.5%, as per resolution of directors, minute book folio....)		

The statement of financial position prepared as at 31 October 2015 is shown below.

Bovine Limited
Statement of Financial Position (extract) as at 31 October 2015

	$NZ
ASSETS	
Current assets	
Bank	487,500
Total assets	$487,500
EQUITY	
Share capital	
500,000 shares fully paid	487,500
Total equity	$487,500

Note

- The number of shares issued must be shown.
- The fact that the shares have been fully paid must be shown. (In some cases shares are partly paid on issue and the balance of the purchase price is paid at a later date. However, these transactions are beyond the scope of this course.)
- The name of the company and the currency used ($NZ) must be shown.

Preliminary Expenses

Preliminary expenses are those expenses that are incurred when a company is first established. They include such items as legal fees, the registration fee with the Companies Office and the preparation, auditing, printing and distribution of the company prospectus. These costs are sometimes known as *formation expenses* or *initial costs*.

NZ IAS 1 (109) recognises that transaction costs relating to equity contributions are not shown in the income statement. They are treated in the same way as brokerage costs – debited directly to equity.

Example 2

Bovine Limited incurred preliminary expenses of $20,000 on 1 September 2015. (Ignore GST.)

Bovine Limited
General Journal

Date	Particulars	Dr $	Cr $
2015 Sep 1	Share capital	20,000	
	Accounts payable		20,000
	(for preliminary expenses incurred)		

Over- and Under-subscription

It would be a very unusual situation indeed if the number of shares applied for was exactly the same as the number on offer. The most likely scenario is that these two numbers would be different.

If there are fewer applications received than shares available, the issue is said to be *undersubscribed*. Undersubscription presents few difficulties – the number of shares issued is the same as the number for which applications have been received.

If applications exceed the number of shares on offer, the issue is said to be *oversubscribed*. In this case the directors must decide which applicants are to receive the shares. The most common scenario is that applications are scaled down in the proportion of the total number of shares available to the total number of applications. For example, if there are twice as many applications as shares available, then each applicant will receive half the number of shares applied for and the balance of the application money will be refunded from the trustee's bank account. This is known as the *pro-rata basis* for allotting shares.

Sometimes, shares will be allotted on a *first-come first-served basis*, in which case all applications received after the issue has been fully subscribed will be rejected. In these cases the unsuccessful applicants' cheques are usually returned unbanked.

Over- or under-subscription for shares does not affect the company's accounting records because all application monies are handled by the trustee.

Example 3

Equine Limited was incorporated on 1 November 2016. On 15 November a prospectus was issued inviting the public to apply for 1,000,000 shares at a price of $2.00 each, payable in full on application. Applications closed on 20 December, by which time applications for 1.5 million shares had been received. The applications were scaled down and shares were allotted on 31 January 2017. Refund cheques were posted the same day. Brokerage was charged at 4% of the proceeds of the issue.

Equine Limited
General Journal

Date	Particulars	Dr $	Cr $
2017 Jan 31	Bank	1,920,000	
	Share capital		1,920,000
	(for the issue of 1,000,000 shares at a price of $2.00 each less brokerage of 4%, as per resolution of directors, minute book folio….)		

The statement of financial position prepared as at 31 January 2017 is shown below.

Equine Limited
Statement of Financial Position (extract) as at 31 January 2017

	$NZ
ASSETS	
Current assets	
Bank	1,920,000
Total assets	$1,920,000
EQUITY	
Share capital	
1,000,000 shares fully paid	1,920,000
Total equity	$1,920,000

QUESTIONS AND TASKS

a   Prepare the general journal entry to record the above.

Aztec Limited
General Journal

b   Prepare the equity section of the statement of financial position as at 30 September 2016.

Aztec Limited
Statement of Financial Position (extract) as at 30 September 2016

2   The directors of *Engineering Equipment Limited*, after incorporation on 1 March 2018, issued a prospectus inviting the public to apply for 600,000 shares at a price of $1.50 per share. The terms of issue specified that the full purchase price was payable on application. When applications closed on 20 March, applications had been received for the exact number of shares on offer. The shares were issued on 31 March and brokerage of 5% was payable. Legal expenses of $9,600 relating to the share issue were paid on 31 March. (Ignore GST)

a   Prepare general journal entries to record the above.

Engineering Equipment Limited
General Journal

2 **b** Prepare the equity section of the statement of financial position as at 31 March 2018.

Engineering Equipment Limited
Statement of Financial Position (extract) as at 31 March 2018

3 On 1 October 2015, *Grand Plans Limited* issued a prospectus inviting the public to apply for 1.6 million shares at an issue price of 75 cents. The terms of issue stated the full amount per share was payable with the application. The closing date for applications was 31 October. By that date applications had been received for the total number of shares on offer. Invoices for incorporation costs of $40,000 (ignore GST) were received on 15 November. The shares were subsequently issued on 30 November and brokerage of 2.5% was payable.

a Prepare general journal entries to record the above.

Grand Plans Limited
General Journal

b Prepare the equity section of the statement of financial position as at 30 November 2015.

Grand Plans Limited
Statement of Financial Position (extract) as at 30 November 2015

4 **This question follows from Question 1.**

The directors of *Aztec Limited* resolved to issue a further 250,000 shares at an issue price of $2.50 through a sharebroker who charges 2.5% brokerage. A prospectus was issued on 1 August 2017. The company was to receive applications for the shares by 31 August, with the terms of issue stating the full purchase price of the shares was payable at the time of application. On the final day for applications, the sharebroker had received applications for 300,000 shares. All applications were scaled down and the shares were allotted on a pro-rata basis and issued on 30 September. No other transactions occurred.

a Prepare the general journal entry to record the above.

Aztec Limited
General Journal

b Prepare the equity section of the statement of financial position as at 30 September 2017.

Aztec Limited
Statement of Financial Position (extract) as at 30 September 2017

5 *Dozo Limited,* after incorporation on 1 February 2016, invited the public to purchase 750,000 shares at $2.00 each. A prospectus was issued, with applications to be made to the company by 20 March. The terms of issue were that the full purchase price of the shares was to be paid with the application. Applications for the full number of shares on offer were received by 10 March. Any applications received after this date were returned to the unsuccessful applicants together with their application cheques which were not banked. Shares were issued on 31 March to the successful applicants. Brokerage costs amounted to 4% of the proceeds of the issue. On 15 April an invoice was received for preliminary expenses of $24,000 (ignore GST).

a Prepare the general journal entries to record the above.

Dozo Limited
General Journal

b Prepare the equity section of the statement of financial position as at 30 April 2016. No further transactions occurred.

Dozo Limited
Statement of Financial Position (extract) as at 30 April 2016

6 On 1 December 2017, *Big Risk Limited* invited the public to apply for 400,000 shares at a price of $3.00 per share. The full price of the shares applied for was to be paid at the time of application. When applications closed on 31 January 2018, the offer had been undersubscribed by 100,000 shares. Shares were issued to applicants on 28 February. Brokerage charges amounted to 5% of the proceeds of the issue.

a Prepare the general journal entry to record the above.

Big Risk Limited
General Journal

b Prepare the equity section of the statement of financial position as at 28 February 2018.

Big Risk Limited
Statement of Financial Position (extract) as at 28 February 2018

7 *Batten Supplies Limited* was incorporated on 1 June 2019. The public was invited to apply for 2 million shares in the company at 50 cents each. Applications closed on 20 August with the full purchase price payable on application. The offer was oversubscribed with applications for 2.2 million shares being received by the closing date. Applications were scaled down and allocated on a pro-rata basis on 31 August. Refund cheques were mailed the same day. Brokerage charges amounted to 4% of the proceeds of the share issue.

Invoices for incorporation costs totalling $48,000 (ignore GST) were received on 30 September.

a Prepare general journal entries to record the above.

Batten Supplies Limited
General Journal

b Prepare the equity section of the statement of financial position as at 30 September 2019.

Batten Supplies Limited
Statement of Financial Position (extract) as at 30 September 2019

Issue of Shares in Exchange for Assets

Sometimes the consideration for the issue of shares takes the form of assets other than cash. For example, a company may issue shares in return for a non-current asset such as a building.

Example 4

On 1 November 2014, Feline Limited issued 100,000 shares with a fair value of $3.00 each in return for land and buildings (valued at $200,000 and $100,000 respectively) owned by Bull Terrier.

Feline Limited
General Journal

Date	Particulars	Dr $	Cr $
2014 Nov 1	Land Buildings Share capital *(for the issue of 100,000 shares with a fair value of $3.00 each to Bull Terrier as consideration for the purchase of land and buildings)*	200,000 100,000	 300,000

Issue of Shares in Satisfaction of Liabilities

Shares may be issued to satisfy liabilities. This transaction has the effect of converting debt finance into permanent equity finance.

Example 5

Canine Limited has a mortgage over its land and buildings of $200,000. The mortgage is held by Mrs A Collie, who is the aunt of the principal shareholder. On 1 July 2017, it was agreed between the company and Mrs Collie that 200,000 shares would be issued in full and final satisfaction of the mortgage. The share issue took place on the same day.

Canine Limited
General Journal

Date	Particulars	Dr $	Cr $
2017 Jul 1	Mortgage – Mrs Collie Share capital *(for the issue of 200,000 shares with a fair value of $1.00 each to Mrs A Collie in full and final satisfaction of the mortgage over land and buildings)*	200,000	 200,000

Debentures

A debenture is a debt instrument whereby a company borrows funds from the public. It is therefore a registered security and is governed by the Securities Act 1978 in the same way as equity securities (shares). A debenture is a form of loan for a fixed period of time at a fixed interest rate. At the end of the time it is repayable by the company to the debenture-holders.

Debentures may be secured or unsecured:

- A **secured** debenture is one that is attached to some or all of the assets of the company. These may be specific assets such as plant and equipment, or the debenture may be a floating charge, which is one that is secured over unspecified assets. The latter is most common because the assets of the company vary from time to time. If the company does not repay the debentures, the assets of the company can be sold to repay them.
- An **unsecured** debenture is not attached to any of the company's assets. If the company fails to repay this type of debenture then the debenture-holders have no more rights than any other unsecured creditor of the company.

Unsecured debentures thus carry greater risk than secured debentures and therefore usually pay a higher rate of interest.

The terms and conditions for the issue of debentures vary considerably. Interest may be payable quarterly, six-monthly, annually, or at the end of the term. Sometimes the debenture-holders may have the option of converting their debentures to shares at the end of the term. In this case the company is converting medium-term debt finance to permanent equity finance.

Debentures may be bought and sold before the end of the term in the same way as shares. The value of the debentures in the marketplace will usually be different from the amount that was first borrowed by the company (the **face value**). Their market value depends on a number of factors:

- the rights attached to the debentures. For example, are they convertible to shares at the end of the term?
- the interest rate compared to current interest rates for similar securities. For example, if interest rates have fallen since the debentures were issued, then the market value of the debenture will often be higher than its face value to reflect the higher return expected.
- the interest accumulated. Interest is paid to the owner of the debenture at the time of the payment. Since interest is paid periodically, interest accrues until the next payment is made. The market value of the debenture may increase above the face value as this interest accrues, and then fall again after the payment has been made.

Under the historical cost measurement base, the carrying amount of a debenture liability in the statement of financial position of the company is its face value. However, if it is converted to equity, then it must be converted at market value. The difference between the face value and the market value is recorded as income or expense at the time of the conversion.

> **REMEMBER!**
>
> Debentures can be bought and sold in the same way as shares.

Example 6

On 31 March 2015, debentures with a carrying amount of $500,000 issued by Lizard Limited were converted into an equivalent market value of ordinary shares. The market value of the debentures was $550,000 and the fair value of the shares was $2.50 per share.

The number of shares issued = $550,000 / $2.50 = 220,000 shares. The difference between the carrying amount and the market value of the debentures is $550,000 − 500,000 = $50,000. Essentially, $500,000 of debt has been converted to $550,000 of equity, resulting in an expense of $50,000. The journal entry to record this event is:

Lizard Limited
General Journal

Date	Particulars	Dr $	Cr $
2015 Mar 31	Debentures Loss on repurchase of debentures Share capital *(for the conversion of debentures to 220,000* *shares with a fair value of $2.50 each)*	500,000 50,000	 550,000

Issue of Shares in Exchange for a Going Concern

The issue of shares by a company to take over a going concern is quite common. For example, the owners of a small business (sole trader or partnership) may decide to form a company to take over their existing business. Company takeovers are commonplace in the commercial marketplace. In many cases the existing shareholders are issued with shares in the company performing the takeover.

The processing of the purchase of a business by a company is very similar to the purchase of a business by a partnership, which was covered earlier.

Example 7

On 1 April 2016, Amphibian Limited agreed to purchase the business of A Frogg, a sporting goods store, in return for the issue of 10,000 shares with a fair value of $2.00 each. The company would take over all assets and liabilities, except the bank and GST accounts, at their carrying amounts, subject to the following:

- Shop fittings are valued at $5,000.
- Of the accounts receivable, $2,000 are considered to be bad debts and a further $1,000 are doubtful.
- Inventory is valued at $15,000.

The statement of financial position of A Frogg immediately prior to the purchase is below.

A Frogg
Statement of Financial Position as at 31 March 2016

	Note	$	$	$
ASSETS				
Non-current assets				
Property, plant and equipment	1			19,000
Current assets				
Bank			3,200	
Accounts receivable			7,500	
Inventory			17,000	
Prepayments			500	
				28,200
Total assets				$47,200
EQUITY AND LIABILITIES				
Non-current liabilities				
Loan from BNZ	2		10,000	
Current liabilities				
Accounts payable		15,000		
GST		2,200		
Total current liabilities			17,200	
Total liabilities				27,200
Equity				
Capital, 31 March 2016				20,000
Total equity and liabilities				$47,200

Notes to the Statement of Financial Position

1 Property, plant and equipment

	Shop fittings $	Van $	Total $
Cost	12,000	25,000	37,000
Accumulated depreciation	8,000	10,000	18,000
Carrying amount	$4,000	$15,000	$19,000

2 Loan from BNZ
The loan has an interest rate of 10% and a maturity date of 30 June 2020.

The general journal entries to record the purchase are:

Amphibian Limited
General Journal

Date	Particulars	Dr $	Cr $
2016	Accounts receivable	5,500	
Apr 1	Inventory	15,000	
	Prepayments	500	
	Shop fittings	5,000	
	Van	15,000	
	Goodwill	5,000	
	Allowance for doubtful debts		1,000
	Accounts payable		15,000
	Loan from BNZ		10,000
	Vendor – A Frogg		20,000
	(for assets and liabilities taken over as per agreement)		

REMEMBER!

Goodwill is the difference between the fair value of the shares issued and the agreed value of the net assets taken over:

$20,000 – 15,000 = $5,000

Amphibian Limited
General Journal (continued)

Date	Particulars	Dr $	Cr $
2016 Apr 1	Vendor – A Frogg Share capital (for the issue of 10,000 shares with a fair value of $2.00 each to Mr A Frogg as consideration for the purchase of his business)	20,000	20,000

Note

- Assets are recorded in the books of the purchasing company at their agreed values. No accumulated depreciation is recorded for property, plant and equipment since the company is a new accounting entity. Thus, where assets are taken over at their carrying amounts, the debit entry in the company's journal is for the net amount. In the above example, the van was taken over at $15,000.
- In the case of accounts receivable, there is still a possibility that doubtful debts may be collected by the company in the future. Thus, although bad debts are not taken over, an allowance is made for any doubtful debts. In the example above, accounts receivable were stated at $7,500 in the accounts of A Frogg. However, of these, $2,000 were bad debts and were not taken over. This left $5,500 ($7,500 – 2,000) of accounts receivable. A further $1,000 were considered doubtful, so an allowance for doubtful debts was created for this amount in the books of the company.
- Liabilities are taken over at the agreed amounts.
- The consideration (shares issued in return for the business) must be at a fair and reasonable value. This is a requirement of the Companies Act 1993.
- Goodwill is calculated as the difference between the agreed value of the net assets and the fair value of the consideration:

Assets	=	$5,500 – 1,000 + 15,000 + 500 + 5,000 + 15,000	=	$40,000
Liabilities	=	$15,000 + 10,000	=	$25,000
Net assets	=	$40,000 – 25,000	=	$15,000
Goodwill	=	Consideration – Net assets		
	=	$20,000 – 15,000 = $5,000		

The Statement of Changes in Equity

Any issues of shares are disclosed in the statement of changes in equity. The total equity is shown in the statement of financial position.

Suppose that, in the above example, *Amphibian Limited* already had share capital of $30,000 (20,000 shares issued at $1.50 each) but had not yet commenced business. The relevant part of the statement of changes in equity would appear as follows:

Statement of Changes in Equity (extract) ...

	Share capital $NZ
Balance at 31 March 2016	30,000
Changes in equity	
Issue of share capital	20,000
Balance at 1 April 2016	$50,000

The Statement of Financial Position

The total number of shares and the dollar amount of share capital must be disclosed in the statement of financial position. However, it is not necessary to disclose the different selling prices of the shares. It is the totals only that must be shown.

Amphibian Limited had already issued 20,000 shares at $1.50 before the purchase of Mr Frogg's business. In return for the business, a further 10,000 shares were issued with a fair value of $2.00 each. The total number of shares on issue is therefore 30,000; the share capital is (20,000 * $1.50 + 10,000 * $2.00) = $50,000.

The equity section of the statement of financial position would appear as follows:

Amphibian Limited
Statement of Financial Position (extract) as at 1 April 2016

	$NZ
Equity	
Share capital	
30,000 shares fully paid	50,000
Total equity	$50,000

KEY POINTS

- A **company** is a separate legal entity registered under the Companies Act 1993.

- The capital of a company is divided into units called **shares**.

- Amounts paid to the company by shareholders are termed **share capital**.

- Shares may be issued to the public upon application on a form contained in the **prospectus**:

  - Cash received with applications for shares must be held by a trustee until either the shares have been issued or the money has been returned to applicants. No entry is made in the company records when applications are received.

  - When shares are issued, the share capital is recorded and the cash (less any brokerage charges) is transferred by the trustee to the company bank account:

Dr	Bank	
Cr		Share capital

  - If the issue is undersubscribed, the number of shares issued is the number applied for. If the issue is oversubscribed, applications are scaled down and a refund is made of excess application monies. No entry is made in the company records to record under- or over-subscription.

- Shares may also be issued:

  - in return for assets (ignoring GST):

Dr	Assets	
Cr		Share capital

  - in satisfaction of liabilities:

Dr	Liability	
Cr		Share capital

  - in return for the purchase of a business as a going concern:

Dr	Assets	
Dr	Goodwill	
Cr		Liabilities
Cr		Share capital

- All shares must be issued at fair value. When a business is purchased as a going concern, the difference between the agreed value of net assets taken over and the fair value of share capital issued is **goodwill**.

- The issue of shares is shown as a separate line in the statement of changes in equity.

- Costs incurred in setting up a company are usually known as **preliminary expenses**. These are not shown in the income statement or statement of comprehensive income, but are debited directly to equity.

QUESTIONS AND TASKS

1   *Turnaround Limited* purchased a building from *Property Developers Limited* on 1 April 2016. The purchase price was $250,000 and the consideration was 125,000 shares with a fair value of $2.00 each.

Prepare the general journal entry to record the purchase of the building in the records of *Turnaround Limited*.

Turnaround Limited
General Journal

2   *Turnaround Limited* had previously purchased another building from *Property Developers Limited*. *Property Developers Limited* held a mortgage of $100,000 over that building. It was agreed on 30 April 2016 that *Property Developers Limited* would accept 50,000 shares in *Turnaround Limited* with a fair value of $2.00 each in full satisfaction of the mortgage.

Prepare the general journal entries to record the above in the records of *Turnaround Limited*.

Turnaround Limited
General Journal

3   On 20 May 2017 *B Williams & Sons Limited* purchased a building from R Abbot. In exchange for the building, 280,000 shares at a price of $1.00 each were issued. *B Williams & Sons* also assumed responsibility for a mortgage on the building. The agreed value of the building was $500,000 and the mortgage was $220,000.

Prepare the general journal entry to record the building purchase in the records of *B Williams & Sons Limited*.

B Williams & Sons Limited
General Journal

4   J McGrath has entered into an agreement to sell a specialised piece of manufacturing equipment to *Tamaki Manufacturing Limited*. The equipment has an historical cost of $200,000 and accumulated depreciation of $40,000. *Tamaki Manufacturing* purchased the equipment at its carrying amount. The consideration given was 320,000 shares at a fair value of 50 cents each. The transaction took place on 11 July 2018, with the shares issued on the same day.

Prepare the general journal entry to record the purchase in the records of *Tamaki Manufacturing Limited*.

Tamaki Manufacturing Limited
General Journal

---

5 On 1 October 2016, *New Wave Investments Limited* invited the public to apply for 400,000 shares at a price of $5.00 per share. The full price of the shares applied for was to be paid at the time of application. When applications closed on 30 November 2016, the offer had been oversubscribed by 200,000 shares. Invoices for accounting costs of $32,000 (ignore GST) relating to the preparation of the prospectus were received on 10 December.

Shares were issued to applicants on 12 December on a first-in first-served basis and application cheques from unsuccessful applicants were returned unbanked. Brokerage charges amounted to 5% of the proceeds of the issue.

On 20 December, the company issued a further 100,000 shares to *Forest Redevelopments Limited* in exchange for a piece of land valued at $450,000.

a Prepare general journal entries to record the above. Narrations are **not** required.

New Wave Investments Limited
General Journal

b Prepare the statement of financial position as at 31 December 2016, assuming no further transactions occurred during December. (Show all items on the face of the statement. Notes are **not** required.)

New Wave Investments Limited
Statement of Financial Position as at 31 December 2016

6 A Cook operates as a sole trader running guided tours. She has decided to convert her business into a company, to be called *A Cook & Company Limited*. The following is the post-closing trial balance of her business as at 31 March 2014:

A Cook
Trial Balance as at 31 March 2014

	$	$
Accounts receivable	10,000	
Bank	6,000	
Vehicles	60,000	
Equipment	16,000	
Allowance for doubtful debts		500
Accounts payable		7,500
Accumulated depreciation – Vehicles		25,000
Accumulated depreciation – Equipment		5,000
GST		2,000
Loan – BankDirect		24,000
A Cook – Capital		28,000
	$92,000	$92,000

The loan from *BankDirect* is interest-only and unsecured, with a fixed interest rate of 7.5% and is due for repayment in full on 31 October 2020.

The new company took over all assets and liabilities, except the GST, at their carrying amounts. The consideration was 30,000 shares issued, with a total value equal to the value of the net assets of the old business. The agreement for sale and purchase is dated 1 April 2014 and the shares were issued the same day.

a Prepare general journal entries to record the above transactions.

A Cook & Company Limited
General Journal

b Prepare the statement of financial position of *A Cook & Company Limited* as at 1 April 2014.

A Cook & Company Limited
Statement of Financial Position as at 1 April 2014

A Cook & Company Limited
Statement of Financial Position (continued) as at 1 April 2014

---

7   *Finance House Limited* had debentures on issue with a face value of $200,000. On 1 March 2015, the company offered the debenture-holders the opportunity to exchange their debentures for fully paid shares in the company. All debenture-holders accepted the offer and the shares were issued on 31 March 2015, when the market value of the debentures was $210,000 and the fair value of the shares was $1.40 each.

Prepare the general journal entry to record the issue of the shares. A **full** narration is required.

Finance House Limited
General Journal

8 On 1 April 2016 *Nationwide Finance Limited* had debentures on issue with a face value of $500,000. On 30 April, the company offered the debenture-holders the opportunity to exchange their debentures for fully paid shares in the company. Half of all debenture-holders accepted this offer and the remainder elected to retain their debentures until maturity. The shares were issued on 31 May 2016, when the fair value of the shares was $4.50 each. Due to an increase in interest rates, the total market value of the debentures had fallen to $450,000 by the time the shares were issued.

Prepare the general journal entry to record the issue of the shares. A **full** narration is required.

Nationwide Finance Limited
General Journal

9 *Viva Limited*, a distributor of pure bottled water, had the following statement of financial position at 30 November 2019:

Viva Limited
Statement of Financial Position as at 30 November 2019

	Note	$NZ	$NZ	$NZ
ASSETS				
Non-current assets				
Property, plant and equipment	1			590,000
Current assets				
Bank			95,000	
Accounts receivable			90,000	
Inventory			180,000	
GST			15,000	
				380,000
Total assets				$970,000
EQUITY AND LIABILITIES				
Non-current liabilities				
Mortgage – BNZ	2		165,000	
Current liabilities				
Accounts payable			85,000	
Total liabilities				250,000
Equity				
Share capital	3			720,000
Total equity and liabilities				$970,000

Notes to the Statement of Financial Position

1 *Property, plant and equipment*

	Cost	Accumulated depreciation	Carrying amount
	$	$	$
Land	370,000	—	370,000
Buildings	220,000	40,000	180,000
Vehicles	65,000	25,000	40,000
	$655,000	$65,000	$590,000

2 *Mortgage*
The mortgage from BNZ is interest-only, with a fixed interest rate of 6.9% and is due for repayment in full on 31 May 2026.

3 *Share capital*
Share capital consists of 600,000 shares fully paid.

On 1 November 2019, *Viva Limited* entered into an agreement to take over a competitor, *Natural H₂O,* as from 30 November 2019. *Natural H₂O* is currently operating as a partnership. The statement of financial position of *Natural H₂O* as at 30 November 2019 is shown opposite.

Natural H₂O
Statement of Financial Position as at 30 November 2019

	Note	$NZ	$NZ	$NZ
ASSETS				
Non-current assets				
Property, plant and equipment	1			333,000
Current assets				
Accounts receivable			120,000	
Inventory			100,000	
				220,000
Total assets				$553,000
EQUITY AND LIABILITIES				
Non-current liabilities				
Loan – Westpac	2		160,000	
Current liabilities				
Bank		80,000		
Accounts payable		70,000		
GST		5,000		
Total current liabilities			155,000	
Total liabilities				315,000
Equity	3			
Capital accounts			150,000	
Current accounts			88,000	
Total equity				238,000
Total equity and liabilities				$553,000

Notes to the Statement of Financial Position

1 Property, plant and equipment	Cost	Accumulated depreciation	Carrying amount
	$	$	$
Plant	180,000	42,000	138,000
Equipment	160,000	25,000	135,000
Vehicles	80,000	20,000	60,000
	$420,000	$87,000	$333,000

2 Loan

The loan from Westpac is interest-only, with a fixed interest rate of 8.5% and is due for repayment in full on 14 September 2022.

3 Equity	Capital	Current	Total equity
	$	$	$
J Roberts	40,000	25,000	65,000
G Roberts	110,000	63,000	173,000
	$150,000	$88,000	$238,000

The purchase was funded by the issue of shares in *Viva Limited* to the partners of *Natural H₂O*. All assets and liabilities were taken over, with the exception of the bank account and GST. The assets of *Natural H₂O* were taken over at their carrying amounts; however an allowance for doubtful debts equal to 2½% of accounts receivable was made.

The purchase took place on 1 December 2019, with shares issued on the same day. *Viva* and *Natural H₂O* agreed on a purchase price of $330,000. *Viva's* shares are to be issued at a price of $1.50, which is their current fair value. Prior to the date of purchase, *Viva Limited* had issued 600,000 shares at $1.20 each.

a Prepare general journal entries to record the purchase of *Natural H₂O* by *Viva Limited*.

Viva Limited
General Journal

b   Prepare the statement of financial position of *Viva Limited* as at 1 December 2019.

Viva Limited
Statement of Financial Position as at 1 December 2019

10 *Extreme Limited*, a retailer of outdoor adventure clothing, had 640,000 shares on issue at $1.00 each. On 1 August 2018, the company invited the public to purchase 100,000 shares in the company at a price of $1.20 each. Applications were to be made, with full payment for the shares, by 20 August. The shares were issued on 31 August.

The share issue was partly intended to fund the purchase of *BackCountry Clothing*, a clothing supplier operating as a sole trader. The statement of financial position of *BackCountry Clothing* as at 15 September 2018 is shown below.

BackCountry Clothing
Statement of Financial Position as at 15 September 2018

	Note	$	$	$
ASSETS				
Non-current assets				
Property, plant and equipment	1			355,000
Current assets				
Accounts receivable			135,000	
Inventory			95,000	
				230,000
Total assets				$585,000
EQUITY AND LIABILITIES				
Non-current liabilities				
Loan	2		145,000	
Current liabilities				
Bank		150,000		
Accounts payable		90,000		
GST		10,000		
Total current liabilities			250,000	
Total liabilities				395,000
Equity				
Capital (15 September 2018)				190,000
Total equity and liabilities				$585,000

Notes to the Statement of Financial Position

1 Property, plant and equipment	Cost	Accumulated depreciation	Carrying amount
	$	$	$
Building	250,000	80,000	170,000
Vehicles	40,000	10,000	30,000
Equipment	200,000	45,000	155,000
	$490,000	$135,000	$355,000

2 *Loan*
The loan from ANZ National Bank is interest-only, with a fixed interest rate of 10.5% and is due for repayment in full on 18 April 2023.

10 continued

On 16 September *Extreme Limited* took over all assets and liabilities of *BackCountry Clothing* with exception of the bank account and GST. The sale and purchase agreement specified that all assets were to be taken over at their carrying amounts, apart from accounts receivable, vehicles and equipment which were to be valued at $125,000, $10,000 and $120,000 respectively. The purchase price of the business was agreed at $300,000, consisting of the issue of 137,500 shares with a fair value of $1.20 per share, with the remainder in cash.

a Prepare general journal entries to record
- the issue of additional shares;
- the purchase of *BackCountry Clothing*; and
- the issue of shares in consideration for the purchase.

Extreme Limited
General Journal

b Prepare the equity section of, and **notes** to, the statement of financial position of *Extreme Limited*.

Extreme Limited
Statement of Financial Position (extract) as at 16 September 2018

Equity	$

Notes to the Statement of Financial Position

11 *Wilson and Wilson Bakers,* operating as a partnership, has recently experienced considerable growth. The partners have decided to form a company, *Tasty Treats Limited,* to operate their snack food business and provide opportunities for expansion. The post-closing trial balance of *Wilson and Wilson Bakers* as at 9 June 2020 is shown below.

Wilson and Wilson Bakers
Trial Balance as at 9 June 2020

	$	$
Accounts receivable	145,000	
Bank	200,000	
Building	440,000	
Factory equipment	640,000	
Inventory	94,000	
Office equipment	45,000	
Accounts payable		186,000
Accumulated depreciation – Buildings		22,000
Accumulated depreciation – Factory equipment		96,000
Accumulated depreciation – Office equipment		28,000
GST		18,000
Loan – BNZ (due 15 January 2018)		264,000
C Wilson – Capital		100,000
C Wilson – Current		400,000
E Wilson – Capital		75,000
E Wilson – Current		375,000
	$1,564,000	$1,564,000

All assets and liabilities of the partnership were taken over on 15 June with the exception of GST and the bank account. The sale and purchase agreement between the company and partnership stipulated that the assets would be valued at their carrying amounts with the following exceptions: inventory $90,000, buildings $450,000 and office equipment $15,000. Goodwill of $28,000 is to be recorded. Accounts receivable is to have $5,000 of bad debts written off and an allowance for doubtful debts created equalling 5% of debtors. The loan from the BNZ will be taken over by the company.

The settlement for the purchase of the partnership was made through the issue of shares with a fair value of 60 cents. The settlement took place on 30 June.

On 1 July 2020, the company offered shares for sale to the public. Applications for the 700,000 available shares closed on 31 July with payment in full due on application. The shares were priced at 60 cents and applications were received for 780,000 shares. Of these, offers to buy 20,000 shares were rejected as payment did not accompany the applications. The remaining shares were issued on a pro-rata basis on 31 August.

Invoices were received on 10 August for preliminary expenses amounting to $6,400 (ignore GST). No other transactions occurred.

a Prepare general journal entries to record the events described above in the accounting records of *Tasty Treats Limited.*

Tasty Treats Limited
General Journal

continued

11 a continued

Tasty Treats Limited
General Journal

b Prepare the **equity** section of, and **notes** to, the statement of financial position of *Tasty Treats Limited.*

Tasty Treats Limited
Statement of Financial Position (extract) as at 31 August 2020

Equity	$

Notes to the Statement of Financial Position

c Prepare the **non-current assets** section of, and **notes** to, the statement of financial position of *Tasty Treats Limited.*

Tasty Treats Limited
Statement of Financial Position (extract) as at 31 August 2020

Non-current assets	$

Notes to the Statement of Financial Position

d Suggest **ONE** reason why **goodwill** was included in the purchase of *Wilson & Wilson Bakers.*

4

YEAR-END EVENTS OF COMPANIES
Accounting for Company Income Tax

Companies are legal entities separate from their owners. This means that they pay their own income tax. The rate of company tax in New Zealand is 30% of taxable income.[2] Income tax is an expense, which is shown in the statement of comprehensive income (or separate income statement, where prepared).

Since the financial year does not end until 31 March, the exact amount of tax for the year is not calculated until the financial statements have been prepared and the taxable income is known. However, companies must pay instalments of tax during the financial year. These instalments are based on an *estimate* of the taxable income for the year and are called *provisional tax* instalments. The payments are normally calculated on the basis of the previous year's taxable income.[3] For companies with a reporting period ending on 31 March, provisional tax instalments are due on 28 August, 15 January and 7 May. The first two payments of provisional tax are treated as a current asset when they are made.

Example 1

a *In the year to 31 March 2015 a company had a taxable income of $90,000. Provisional tax payments were made on the due dates in the following year.*

The total amount of provisional tax payable for the year ended 31 March 2016 is equal to 105% of the tax on $90,000: 105% x (30% x $90,000) = $28,350. This amount is payable in three equal instalments of $28,350/3 = $9,450. These payments are recorded as follows:

General Journal

Date	Particulars	Dr $	Cr $
2015 Aug 28	Provisional tax paid Bank *(cash payments journal entry)*	9,450	9,450
2016 Jan 15	Provisional tax paid Bank *(cash payments journal entry)*	9,450	9,450
May 7	Income tax payable Bank *(cash payments journal entry)*	9,450	9,450

At the end of the reporting period, the taxable income is determined and the correct amount of income tax expense is calculated. By the time the third instalment of provisional tax is paid, the liability account for income tax payable has been credited. The third instalment is therefore debited against this liability.

b *In the example above, taxable income for the year to 31 March 2016 was $120,000.*

The total tax payable is equal to 30% of the taxable income: 30% * $120,000 = $36,000. However, the company has already paid provisional tax of $28,350 for the 2016 financial year. The amount of tax still owing is thus: $36,000 − 28,350 = $7,650. This amount is called *terminal tax* and is due for payment on 7 February 2017.

---

[2] It is important to note that there is a difference between taxable income and the profit before tax that is reported in the statement of comprehensive income (or separate income statement where prepared). Differences arise for many reasons, for example: doubtful debts is an expense for accounting purposes but may not be treated as an expense for tax purposes; the Inland Revenue Department has specified depreciation rates which are often different from the depreciation rates that are used for accounting purposes.

[3] This method of calculating provisional tax is known as the *standard* option, where the previous year's taxable income is used as the base. Total provisional tax to be paid is 105% of the tax payable on the previous year's taxable income. There is an alternative method that can be used, whereby the company estimates its taxable income for the year and pays provisional tax on that basis. However, there are penalties for paying insufficient provisional tax, so great care must be taken if this option is chosen.

Provisional tax payments for the 2017 year (due on 28 August 2016 and 15 January and 7 May 2017) will each be one-third of 30% * $120,000 * 105% = $12,600.

The time line below shows the relationships between the financial year and the timing of provisional and terminal tax payments.

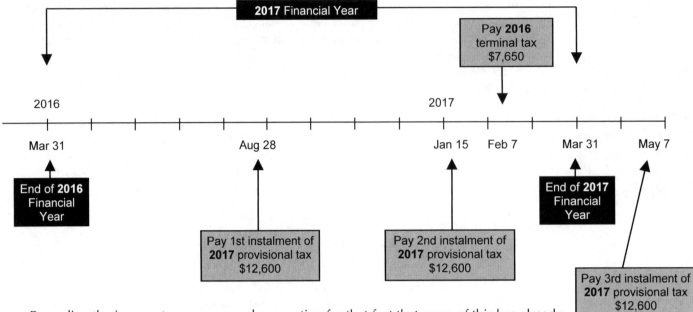

Recording the income tax expense and accounting for that fact that some of this has already been paid requires two journal entries:

i Record the income tax expense

General Journal

Date	Particulars	Dr $	Cr $
2016 Mar 31	Income tax expense	36,000	
	Income tax payable[4]		36,000
	(to record income tax expense for the year)		

ii Close the provisional tax paid account

General Journal

Date	Particulars	Dr $	Cr $
2016 Mar 31	Income tax payable	18,900	
	Provisional tax paid		18,900
	(to offset provisional tax paid during the year)		

The relevant ledger accounts would now appear as follows:

General Ledger
Provisional Tax Paid   1050

Date	Particulars	Ref	Dr $	Cr $	Balance $
2015 Aug 28	Bank	CPJ1	9,450		9,450 Dr
2016 Jan 15	Bank	CPJ1	9,450		18,900 Dr
Mar 31	Income tax payable	GJ1		18,900	—

---

4   In some older texts, this account would be named Provision for Taxation. However, *NZ IAS 37 (10)* defines a provision as *a liability of uncertain timing or amount*. Since the amount of tax can be calculated and the timing is clear, there is rarely any justification for labelling the tax liability as a provision.

Date	Particulars	Ref	Dr $	Cr $	Balance $	
2016						
Mar 31	Income tax expense	GJ1		36,000	36,000	Cr
	Provisional tax paid	GJ1	18,900		17,100	Cr
May 7	Bank	CPJ1	9,450		7,650	Cr

At 31 March, the balance of the income tax payable account is $17,100, which represents the final payment of provisional tax ($9,450) together with the terminal tax of $7,650 due on 7 February 2017.[5] The provisional tax is paid on 7 May, leaving only the terminal liability.

The income tax expense account is just another expense for the year, which should be closed to the income summary account at the end of the year:

General Journal

Date	Particulars	Dr $	Cr $
2016	Income summary	36,000	
Mar 31	Income tax expense		36,000
	(closing entry)		

Overpaid Provisional Tax

If the taxable income for the year is determined to be less than 105% of the previous year's taxable income, the company will have paid too much provisional tax. This means that, rather than having to make a terminal tax payment on 7 February of the following year, the company is entitled to a refund of the overpayment.

In practical terms, however, most companies do not bother to ask for their overpayment to be refunded. Instead, they ask Inland Revenue to hold the overpayment against the provisional tax due for the following year. The reason for this is that the financial statements have often only just been completed when the first provisional tax payment is due on 28 August. If there is a refund due from the previous year, it is much easier to ask Inland Revenue to transfer the balance from one year to another than to ask for a refund and then have to pay the provisional tax instalment. Consider the following situation:

Example 2

In Example 1 above, taxable income for the year to 31 March 2016 was $72,000.

The tax payable is equal to 30% of the taxable income: 30% * $72,000 = $24,000. The company has already paid provisional tax of $18,900 for the 2016 financial year. The journal entries are:

i   Record the income tax expense

General Journal

Date	Particulars	Dr $	Cr $
2016	Income tax expense	24,000	
Mar 31	Income tax payable		24,000
	(to record income tax expense for the year)		

ii   Close the provisional tax paid account

General Journal

Date	Particulars	Dr $	Cr $
2016	Income tax payable	18,900	
Mar 31	Provisional tax paid		18,900
	(to offset provisional tax paid during the year)		

---

[5]   The income tax payable is a current liability. However, since the tax is not due to be paid until 7 February it should be excluded from any calculation of the liquid ratio.

A third provisional instalment of $9,450 is due and payable on 7 May 2016. Once this instalment has been paid, the amount of tax overpaid will be $28,350 – $24,000 = $4,350. The income tax payable account will then have a **debit** balance, representing the amount owed by Inland Revenue to the company:

General Ledger

Income Tax Payable   3250

Date	Particulars	Ref	Dr $	Cr $	Balance $	
2016						
Mar 31	Income tax expense	GJ1		24,000	24,000	Cr
	Provisional tax paid	GJ1	18,900		5,100	Cr
May 7	Bank	CPJ1	9,450		4,350	Dr

> **REMEMBER!**
>
> A company may choose to offset a tax refund against the following year's provisional tax due.

Remember, the company has two options: it can elect to have the overpaid amount refunded by Inland Revenue, or it can offset this amount against the first instalment of provisional tax for the following year.

The refund option is a straightforward entry in the cash receipts journal. If the company elects to offset the overpayment, the amount must be transferred back to the provisional tax paid account because it now represents provisional tax that has been paid for the 2017 year:

General Journal

Date	Particulars	Dr $	Cr $
2016	Provisional tax paid	4,350	
Aug 28	Income tax payable		4,350
	(to offset tax refund due from 2013 against 2014 provisional tax due)		

If we carry the example one step further, we can work out the amounts of provisional tax that the company will have to pay during the 2017 financial year.

Remember that the total amount of provisional tax payable equals 105% of the total tax payable on the taxable income of the previous financial year. In the 2016 year, taxable income was $72,000 and the tax payable on this amounted to $21,600. The total provisional tax due in the 2017 year is thus 105% * $21,600 = $22,680.

Under normal circumstances, the company would pay one-third of this amount ($22,680/3 = $7,560) on each of 28 August 2016, 15 January 2017 and 7 May 2017. However, it has overpaid the previous year's provisional tax by $4,350, so this amount will be offset against the provisional tax instalment due on 28 August 2016. On this date, the company would pay $3,210 ($7,560 – 4,350). The instalments on each of 15 January and 7 May 2017 would remain at $7,560. The journal entries to record these payments would thus be:

General Journal

Date	Particulars	Dr $	Cr $
2016	Provisional tax paid	3,210	
Aug 28	Bank		3,210
	(cash payments journal entry)		
2017	Provisional tax paid	7,560	
Jan 15	Bank		7,560
	(cash payments journal entry)		
May 7	Income tax payable	7,560	
	Bank		7,560
	(cash payments journal entry)		

Disclosure of Income Tax in the Financial Statements

- Income tax is an expense that is shown in the statement of comprehensive income (or separate income statement where prepared). It is usual to show the profit before taxation, then deduct the income tax expense and show the tax-paid profit separately:

Income Statement (extract)[6] for the year ended 31 March 2016

		$NZ
Income		150,000
Less:	Expenses	78,000
Profit before taxation		72,000
Less:	Taxation expense	21,600
Profit for the year		$50,400

- The income tax payable is a current liability unless there has been an overpayment of provisional tax in which case it has a debit balance and is a current asset. This would require that the first two instalments of provisional tax are greater than the total income tax payable for the year, so would arise only where there has been a reduction in taxable income of almost one-third compared to the previous year.

Closing Entries

After closing entries for income and expenses (including income tax) have been prepared and posted to the ledger, the balance of the income summary account represents the profit (or loss) for the period. At the end of the reporting period the income summary account is closed to the *retained earnings* account in the general ledger. The tax-paid profit for the year is thus transferred to this account.

The *retained earnings* account is an equity account, which effectively represents the accumulated profits of the company to date. Dividends paid to shareholders are debited to this account, as we will see later in this section.

Example 3

At 1 April 2014, Reptile Limited had share capital of $800,000, being 1,600,000 fully paid shares, and retained earnings of $150,000. The company recorded income of $500,000 and expenses of $260,000 in the year ended 31 March 2015. The company tax rate is 30%.

The journal entries to record the income tax expense and to close the income summary account are as follows:

Reptile Limited
General Journal

Date	Particulars	Dr $	Cr $
2015 Mar 31	Income tax expense	72,000	
	Income tax payable		72,000
	*(to record income tax expense for the year [30% * ($500,000 – 260,000)])*		
	Income	500,000	
	Income summary		500,000
	(closing entry)		
	Income summary	332,000	
	Expenses		260,000
	Income tax expense		72,000
	(closing entry)		
	Income summary	168,000	
	Retained earnings		168,000
	(closing entry)		

---

[6] For simplicity, this example assumes that the profit is the same amount as the taxable income for the year. Under most circumstances this would not be the case.

The retained earnings account in the general ledger appears as follows:

General Ledger

Retained Earnings   5300

Date	Particulars	Ref	Dr $	Cr $	Balance $	
2014 Apr 1	Balance	b/d			150,000	Cr
2015 Mar 31	Income summary	GJ1		168,000	318,000	Cr

A summary income statement is as follows:

Reptile Limited
Income Statement (extract) for the year ended 31 March 2015

	$NZ
Income	500,000
Less: Expenses	260,000
Profit before taxation	240,000
Less: Taxation expense	72,000
Profit	$168,000

The equity section of the statement of financial position is:

Reptile Limited
Statement of Financial Position (extract) as at 31 March 2015

Equity	Note	$NZ000	$NZ000
Share capital	1	800	
Retained earnings		318	
Total equity			1,118

Notes to the Statement of Financial Position
1 *Share capital*
Issued capital consists of 1,600,000 shares fully paid.

Other Company Expenses

1 Companies have some expenses that are peculiar to the company form of organisation. For example, most companies are required to have their accounts audited and thus audit fees are payable. Many companies pay fees to the directors for their work in running the company.

The recording of these expenses is exactly the same as for any other type of expense.

2 Writing down Inventory
NZ IAS 2 (9) requires that inventory is measured at the lower of cost and net realisable value. Thus, if the expected realisable value is lower than the cost, there will be an amount of inventory that must be written down. For example, suppose that inventory of high-fashion clothing cost $8,000 but is now expected to sell for no more than $5,000. The journal entry to adjust the inventory value is:

General Journal

Date	Particulars	Dr $	Cr $
Mar 31	Inventory write-down Inventory *(to record inventory written down to net realisable value)*	3,000	3,000

> **REMEMBER!**
>
> Inventory is shown in the statement of financial position at the lower of cost and net realisable value.

Disclosure
- An inventory write-down forms part of the cost of goods sold expense and is shown separately in the statement of comprehensive income (or separate income statement, where prepared).

QUESTIONS AND TASKS

1 *Oakura Holdings Limited* recorded income of $60,000 and expenses of $45,000 in the year to 30 June 2016. The company tax rate is 30% of the pre-tax profit.

Prepare general journal entries to record
- the income tax expense for the year; and
- closing entries for income, expenses and the income summary account.

Oakura Holdings Limited
General Journal

2 *Whangaruru Waterways Limited* reported a pre-tax profit of $40,000 in the year to 31 March 2017. The company paid provisional tax of $10,500, in equal instalments on 28 August 2016, 15 January 2017 and 7 May 2017. The company tax rate is 30% of the pre-tax profit.

a Prepare general journal entries to record
- the income tax expense for the year to 31 March 2017; and
- closing entries for income tax expense, provisional tax paid and the income summary account.

Whangaruru Waterways Limited
General Journal

continued

2 a continued   **Whangaruru Waterways Limited**
                                  General Journal (continued)

b Prepare the following ledger accounts up to **31 March 2017**:

Whangaruru Waterways Limited
General Ledger

Provisional Tax Paid

Income Tax Expense

Income Tax Payable

---

3 The provisional tax paid account in the ledger of *Teal Bay Boating Limited* had a balance of $20,000 Dr on 31 March 2018. One further $10,000 instalment of provisional tax is due on 7 May 2018. The company tax on the profit for the year amounts to $28,600.

a Prepare general journal entries **without narrations** to record
- the company income tax expense for the year to 31 March 2018;
- the transfer of provisional tax paid; and
- the payment of the third instalment of provisional tax.

Teal Bay Boating Limited
General Journal

b Prepare the following ledger accounts up to **30 June 2018**:

Teal Bay Boating Limited
General Ledger
Provisional Tax Paid

Income Tax Expense

Income Tax Payable

c Explain the situation regarding the company's terminal tax for the year.

_____

_____

_____

_____

_____

_____

---

4 The provisional tax paid account in the ledger of *Mokau Manufacturers Limited* had a balance of $27,000 Dr on 31 March 2018. The company pays its provisional tax in three equal instalments on 28 August, 15 January and 7 May. Pre-tax profit for the year to 31 March 2018 was $150,000. The company tax rate is 30% of the pre-tax profit. Provisional tax is payable for the following year at 105% of the current year's tax expense.

For the year to 31 March 2019, all provisional tax payments were made on time, on 28 August 2018, and on 15 January and 7 May 2019. The 2018 terminal tax was paid on 7 February 2019. The pre-tax profit for the year ended 31 March 2019 was $120,000.

a Prepare the journal entries **without narrations** to record
- income tax expense for the year ended 31 March 2018
- transfer of provisional tax at 31 March 2018
- closing the income summary account at 31 March 2018
- payment of the third instalment of provisional tax for the year ended 31 March 2018
- payment of the first two instalments of provisional tax for the 2019 financial year
- payment of 2018 terminal tax
- income tax expense for the year ended 31 March 2019
- transfer of provisional tax at 31 March 2019
- closing the income summary account at 31 March 2019.

Mokau Manufacturers Limited
General Journal

continued

4　a　continued　　　　　　　　　**Mokau Manufacturers Limited**
General Journal (continued)

b　Prepare the ledger accounts below for the period **1 April 2017 to 31 March 2019**.

Mokau Manufacturers Limited
General Ledger

Provisional Tax Paid

Income Tax Expense

Mokau Manufacturers Limited
General Ledger

Income Tax Payable

c   After the final provisional payment has been made on 7 May 2019, the income tax payable account will have a *debit* balance. Describe the company's position regarding **terminal tax** for the year ended 31 March 2019. You should:

- **calculate** the balance of the income tax payable account after the payment on 7 May;
- **explain** the circumstances that gave rise to the debit balance; and
- **explain** the options available to the company.

_____
_____
_____
_____
_____
_____
_____
_____
_____
_____
_____
_____
_____
_____
_____
_____

---

5   *Ruakaka Traders Limited* has inventory on hand which cost $25,000 (excluding GST) at 31 March 2017. However, of this, inventory costing $5,000 is now expected to sell for $1,500 (excluding GST).

a   Prepare the journal entry to account for the change in inventory.

General Journal

b   Prepare the extract from the statement of financial position to show how inventory would appear at 31 March 2017.

_____
_____
_____

Accounting for Dividends

Dividends are amounts paid to shareholders that do not result in the reduction of their capital investment. Traditionally, dividends have been regarded as a share of company profits paid to shareholders, but this is not always the case. Dividends may be paid from any part of equity.

Since a company usually waits until the profit for the year is known before a final dividend is recommended, the dividend for a particular reporting period is declared after the end of the period. At the end of the reporting period, then, the amount of the dividend is unknown and since it has not been declared, the amount of the final dividend is not a liability of the company. However, during the year, the company may have paid an interim dividend, which is similar to an instalment on the final dividend. Any interim dividend that has been paid represents a payment to shareholders and will therefore affect equity. Consider the example below.

Example 4

Whale Limited *issued 100,000 shares with a total share capital of $500,000 on 1 July 2014. The tax-paid profit for the year to 30 June 2015 was $400,000 and the company paid an interim dividend of 5 cents per share on 20 December 2014. In July 2015 a final dividend of 10 cents per share was declared. This dividend was paid on 13 August 2015.*

The only dividend to be reported in the financial statements at 30 June 2015 is the payment of the interim dividend which was made in December 2014. The journal entry to record this transaction is as follows:

General Journal

Date	Particulars	Dr $	Cr $
2014 Dec 20	Interim dividend	5,000	
	Bank		5,000
	(cash payments journal entry)		

At the end of the reporting period the interim dividend account is closed to the retained earnings account:

General Journal

Date	Particulars	Dr $	Cr $
2015 Jun 30	Retained earnings	5,000	
	Interim dividend		5,000
	(closing entry)		

The payment of the final dividend is recorded when it is made in August:

General Journal

Date	Particulars	Dr $	Cr $
2015 Aug 13	Final dividend	10,000	
	Bank		10,000
	(cash payments journal entry)		

Disclosure
- The interim dividend paid is disclosed in retained earnings column of the statement of changes in equity for the year ended 30 June 2015:

Whale Limited
Statement of Changes in Equity for the year ended 30 June 2015

	Share capital $NZ000	Retained earnings $NZ000	Total equity $NZ000
Balance at 1 July 2014	500	—	500
Changes in equity for 2015			
Dividends paid		(5)	(5)
Total comprehensive income for the year		400	400
Balance at 30 June 2015	**500**	**395**	**895**

■ The declaration of the final dividend has no effect on equity:

Statement of Financial Position (extract) as at 30 June 2015

Equity	Note	$NZ000	$NZ000
Share capital	1	500	
Retained earnings		395	
Total equity			895

Notes to the Statement of Financial Position
1 *Share capital*
   Issued capital consists of 100,000 shares fully paid

■ The final dividend is not shown as a liability in the financial statements prepared at 30 June 2015 because it was declared after the end of the reporting period[7]. However, since it will have an influence on the decision-making process of users, it must be disclosed as a note to the financial statements. Both the dividend per share and the total amount of dividend payable must be shown. For example:

> *A final dividend of 10 cents per share, amounting to a total of $10,000, was proposed in July 2015.*

Example 5

This example follows from Example 4.
In the year ended 30 June 2016, the company reported a tax-paid profit of $500,000. An interim dividend of 7 cents per share had been paid on 21 December 2015 and a final dividend of 12 cents per share was declared in July 2016 and paid on 15 August.

The payment of the final dividend for 2015 is shown as:

General Journal

Date	Particulars	Dr $	Cr $

2015 Aug 13	Final dividend
	    Bank
	    (cash payments journal entry)
		10,000	10,000

The payment of the interim dividend for 2016 is shown as:

General Journal

Date	Particulars	Dr $	Cr $

2015 Dec 21	Interim dividend
	    Bank
	    (cash payments journal entry)
		7,000	7,000

At the end of the reporting period both the final dividend account (which shows the dividend for 2015) and the interim dividend account are closed to retained earnings:

---

[7] NZ IAS 10 (12): "If an entity declares dividends to holders of equity instruments after the end of the reporting period, the entity shall not recognise those dividends as a liability at the end of the reporting period."

General Journal

Date	Particulars	Dr $	Cr $
2016 Jun 30	Retained earnings	17,000	
	Final dividend		10,000
	Interim dividend		7,000
	(closing entry)		

The financial statements appear as follows:

Whale Limited
Statement of Changes in Equity for the year ended 30 June 2016

	Share capital $NZ000	Retained earnings $NZ000	Total equity $NZ000
Balance at 1 July 2015	500	395	895
Changes in equity for 2016			
Dividends		(17)	(17)
Total comprehensive income for the year		500	500
Balance at 30 June 2016	**500**	**878**	**1,378**

The dividends paid are the final dividend for 2015 of $10,000 and the interim dividend for 2016 of $7,000.

Statement of Financial Position (extract) as at 30 June 2016

Equity	Note	$NZ000	$NZ000
Share capital	1	500	
Retained earnings		878	
Total equity			1,378

Notes to the Statement of Financial Position

1   *Share capital*
    Issued share capital consists of 100,000 shares fully paid

NOTE:
A final dividend of 12 cents per share, amounting to a total of $12,000, was proposed in July.

The Solvency Test

Before a company is permitted to pay a cash dividend, it must meet the requirements of the **Solvency Test** as prescribed by s 4(1) of the Companies Act 1993. A company satisfies the solvency test if, after the dividend has been paid:

(a)   the company is able to pay its debts as they become due in the ordinary course of business; and

(b)   the value of the company's assets is greater than the value of its liabilities including contingent liabilities.

It is important to note that these requirements must be met **after** the payment of the dividend. This is very important because it protects the interests of outside parties.

Part (a) is often known as the **liquidity leg** of the solvency test. It is designed to protect the interests of creditors in that it prevents a company from paying dividends if, by doing so, it would then be unable to meet its normal business debts.

Part (b) is often called the **balance sheet** test. Essentially this test means that, after the distribution, the company must have positive equity. It is important to note that contingent liabilities must also be taken into account in this leg of the solvency test. This means that, should there be a contingent liability, the probability of it becoming a reality should be assessed. If meeting the contingent liability would result in the company having negative equity, then a dividend should not be paid.

If a company pays a dividend but does not meet the requirements of the solvency test, then the directors can be held personally liable for any amounts paid to shareholders that were needed to satisfy creditors at the time the dividend was paid.

REMEMBER!

■ An *interim dividend* is paid during the current year in anticipation of the year's profit.

■ A *final dividend* is declared after year end and is paid in the following financial year.

KEY POINTS

- Companies are separate legal entities and pay their own income tax.

  - Companies pay provisional tax in three instalments throughout the year. The first two instalments (28 August and 15 January) are recorded as:

    Dr Provisional tax paid
    Cr   Bank

  - At the end of the year the actual tax liability is calculated:

    Dr   Income tax expense
    Cr   Income tax payable

  - The provisional tax that has been paid is closed against the tax liability:

    Dr   Income tax payable
    Cr   Provisional tax paid

  - The third instalment of provisional tax (7 May) is debited against the tax liability:

    Dr   Income tax payable
    Cr   Bank

  - The balance in the income tax payable account is known as **terminal tax**. If the account is in debit, then provisional tax has been overpaid and a refund is due to the company.

  - The income tax expense is closed to the income summary account:

    Dr   Income summary
    Cr   Income tax expense

- At the end of the reporting period, the income summary account is closed to the retained earnings account which forms part of equity:

    Dr   Income summary
    Cr   Retained earnings

- Payments made to shareholders are known as **dividends**.

  - Companies normally pay dividends from retained earnings, i.e. from the company tax-paid profit.

  - Dividends paid during the year in advance of the year's profit are known as **interim dividends**:

    Dr   Interim dividend paid
    Cr   Bank

  - A **final dividend** is based on the tax-paid profit for the year. It is declared after the end of the reporting period and cannot be paid until it has been approved by shareholders at the annual general meeting of the company.

    Dr   Final dividend paid
    Cr   Bank

  - A proposed dividend is not a liability, so it cannot be shown in the financial statements until it has been paid. However, the company's intention to pay a dividend must be disclosed as a note to the financial statements.

  - All dividends **paid** during the year (normally the final dividend for the *previous* year and the interim dividend for the *current* year) are closed to retained earnings at the end of the year:

    Dr   Retained earnings
    Cr   Interim/Final dividend paid

- Dividends paid are shown under in the statement of changes in equity.

- Payment of dividends is subject to the **solvency test**.

QUESTIONS AND TASKS

1 On 1 April 2015 *Siesta Beds Limited* had total share capital of $1,000,000, consisting of 1,000,000 shares, and retained earnings of $410,000. An interim dividend of 3 cents per share was paid on 30 August 2015. For the year ended 31 March 2016, the company reported a net tax-paid profit of $100,000. A proposed final dividend of 5 cents per share was announced on 14 June 2016.

a Prepare general journal entries to record
- the payment of the interim dividend; and
- closing entries for the interim dividend and the income summary account.

Siesta Beds Limited
General Journal

b Prepare the retained earnings account in the general ledger.

Siesta Beds Limited
General Ledger

Retained Earnings

c Prepare the equity section of the statement of financial position as at 31 March 2016, **and related notes**.

Siesta Beds Limited
Statement of Financial Position (extract) as at 31 March 2016

Equity	Note	$NZ	$NZ
Share capital	1		
Retained earnings			
Total equity			

Notes to the Statement of Financial Position

1 *Share capital*

1 **d** Prepare a note to show how the proposed final dividend should be disclosed.

_____

_____

_____

_____

2 On 1 July 2017 _Karaoke Hire Company Limited_ had total share capital of $550,000, representing 110,000 shares, and retained earnings of $42,000. The following events took place:

Date	
30 September 2017:	Paid final dividend of 14 cents per share for the year ended 30 June 2017
31 January 2018:	Paid interim dividend of 18 cents per share for the year ended 30 June 2018
20 August 2018:	Tax-paid profit of $44,000 and proposed final dividend of 20 cents per share announced for the year ended 30 June 2018.

a Prepare general journal entries to record
- the payment of dividends; and
- closing entries for the dividend and income summary accounts.

Karaoke Hire Company Limited
General Journal

b Prepare the retained earnings account in the general ledger.

Karaoke Hire Company Limited
General Ledger
Retained Earnings

c Prepare the equity section of the statement of financial position as at 30 June 2018, **and related notes**.

Karaoke Hire Company Limited
Statement of Financial Position (extract) as at 30 June 2018

Equity	Note	$NZ	$NZ
Share capital	1		
Retained earnings			
Total equity			

Notes to the Statement of Financial Position

1 *Share capital*

---

3 At 1 April 2017, *Chromium Finishing Limited* had total issued share capital of $19,800,000, which consisted of 900,000 fully-paid shares. Retained earnings were $2,700,000. The following events occurred over the next two years:

Date	
30 November 2017	Paid interim dividend of 40 cents per share for the year ended 31 March 2018
30 April 2018	Tax-paid profit of $1.8 million and proposed final dividend of $1.50 per share announced for the year ended 31 March 2018
15 July 2018	Paid final dividend announced on 30 April
30 November 2018	Paid interim dividend of 75 cents per share for the year ended 31 March 2019
31 December 2018	Issued a further 100,000 shares at $25 per share
31 May 2019	Tax-paid profit of $1.6 million and proposed final dividend of $1.00 per share announced for the year ended 31 March 2019. All shareholders are entitled to participate in this dividend.

a Prepare general journal entries, including closing entries, to record the above events. Narrations are **not** required.

Chromium Finishing Limited
General Journal

3 **b** Prepare the retained earnings account for the period 1 April 2017 to 31 March 2019.

Chromium Finishing Limited
General Ledger

Retained Earnings

c Prepare the statement of changes in equity for the year ended 31 March 2019.

Chromium Finishing Limited
Statement of Changes in Equity for the year ended 31 March 2019

	Share capital $	Retained earnings $	Total equity $
Balance at 1 April 2018			
Changes in equity for 2019			
Issue of share capital			
Dividends			
Total comprehensive income for the year			
Balance at 31 March 2019			

d Prepare the equity section of the statement of financial position as at 31 March 2019, **and related notes**.

Chromium Finishing Limited
Statement of Financial Position (extract) as at 31 March 2019

Equity			

Notes to the Statement of Financial Position

1 *Share capital*

_____

_____

e Prepare a note to show how the proposed final dividend should be disclosed.

_____

_____

_____

4 At 1 April 2016, *Wooden Trinkets Limited* had 120,000 fully-paid shares on issue, with an average issue price of $1.50 each. Retained earnings were $30,000. On 30 November 2016, 30,000 further shares were issued at $2.00 each. The following entries have been extracted from the company's journals for the year ended 31 March 2017:

Wooden Trinkets Limited
General Journal (extract)

Date	Particulars	Dr $	Cr $
2016 Jun 25	Final dividend	12,000	
	Bank		12,000
Aug 28	Provisional tax paid	17,000	
	Income tax payable		10,000
	Bank		7,000
Nov 30	Interim dividend	6,000	
	Bank		6,000
Dec 31	Inventory write-down	7,500	
	Inventory		7,500
2017 Mar 31	Income summary	23,000	
	Retained earnings		23,000

a **Fully explain** the transactions that gave rise to the journal entries on the following dates:

June 25 _____

_____

August 28 _____

_____

November 28 _____

_____

December 31 _____

_____

March 31 _____

_____

b Prepare the closing entry or entries required for **dividends** at 31 March 2017. Narrations are **not** required.

Wooden Trinkets Limited
General Journal

c Prepare the statement of changes in equity for the year ended 31 March 2017.

Wooden Trinkets Limited
Statement of Changes in Equity for the year ended 31 March 2017

	Share capital $	Retained earnings $	Total equity $
Balance at 1 April 2016			
Changes in equity for 2017			
Issue of share capital			
Dividends			
Total comprehensive income for the year			
Balance at 31 March 2017			

5

OTHER COMPANY TRANSACTIONS
Repurchase of Shares

A company may decide to repurchase its own shares for many reasons. Some of these are:

- The company may have excess cash and perceive that buying its own shares is the best way to invest this cash.
- The company may wish to drive up its share price to enhance its market image and do so by creating a demand for its shares in the market.
- The company may wish to strengthen its dividend flow and can do this by reducing the number of shares on issue so that the same total dividend is paid on fewer shares.

A company may not repurchase its own shares unless it meets the requirements of the solvency test in the same way as it must do before dividends are paid.

The simplest scenario occurs when a company repurchases shares at their issue price. In this case, the journal entry required is essentially the reverse of that which was prepared when the shares were issued, and has the effect of cancelling the share capital.

Example 1

At 31 March 2016 a company had 500,000 shares on issue. These shares had been issued at $2.00. On 30 April 2016 the company repurchased 50,000 of these shares at $2.00 each.

The journal entry to record the repurchase is:

General Journal

Date	Particulars	Dr $	Cr $
2016 Apr 30	Share capital	100,000	
	Bank		100,000
	(for the repurchase of 50,000 shares at $2.00 per share)		

During the course of a company's life, it is more likely that shares will be issued at different prices. Under these circumstances, there are different ways of recording the repurchase of shares. Here we will concern ourselves with only one approach, which is to use the weighted average of the share issue prices to determine the amount of share capital being repurchased. If the price paid is less than this weighted average, then there is a gain on the repurchase which is credited to retained earnings. Conversely, if the price paid for the repurchased shares is greater than the weighted average issue price, the company has effectively made a loss on the repurchase. This loss is debited to retained earnings.

Example 2

At 31 March 2015 Dolphin Limited *had 200,000 shares on issue. These shares had been issued at the following prices: 100,000 at $3.00, 50,000 at $3.20 and 50,000 at $3.80. Retained earnings amounted to $150,000. On 10 April 2015 the company repurchased 20,000 of its shares at $4.00 per share.*

Before the repurchase can be recorded, we must calculate the weighted average issue price of the shares:

Number of shares	Issue price	Total
100,000	$3.00	$300,000
50,000	3.20	160,000
50,000	3.80	190,000
200,000		$650,000

The weighted average issue price is therefore $650,000 / 200,000 = $3.25 per share.

The company has paid $4.00 for each of the shares. This means that, in the repurchase, each share is costing an average of 75 cents more than was received when it was sold. This represents a loss to the company:

- The amount of share capital which has been repurchased is: 20,000 shares @ $3.25 per share = $65,000.
- The amount of the loss is: 20,000 shares @ $0.75 per share = $15,000.
- The amount of cash paid is: 20,000 shares @ $4.00 per share = $80,000.

The amount of the loss on repurchase is recorded against retained earnings. The journal entry to record the repurchase is:

Dolphin Limited
General Journal

Date	Particulars	Dr $	Cr $
2015 Apr 10	Share capital	65,000	
	Retained earnings	15,000	
	Bank		80,000
	(for the repurchase of 20,000 shares at $4.00 per share)		

Disclosure

The repurchase of shares is shown in the statement of changes in equity:

Dolphin Limited
Statement of Changes in Equity for the period 1 April to 10 April 2015

	Share capital $NZ000	Retained earnings $NZ000	Total equity $NZ000
Balance at 1 April 2015	650	150	800
Changes in equity for 2015			
Repurchase of share capital	(65)	(15)	(80)
Balance at 10 April 2015	**585**	**135**	**720**

Statement of Financial Position (extract) as at 10 April 2015

Equity	Note	$NZ000
Share capital	1	585
Retained earnings		135
Total equity		**$720**

Notes to the Statement of Financial Position
1 *Share capital*
Issued capital consists of 180,000 shares fully paid.

Example 3

Suppose, in the previous example, that the company repurchased its shares for $2.75 each.

In this case *Dolphin Limited* is paying $2.75 for each share that it originally sold for an average price of $3.25. Thus a gain of 50 cents per share is made which will be transferred to retained earnings. The entry to record the repurchase is:

Dolphin Limited
General Journal

Date	Particulars	Dr $	Cr $
2015 Apr 10	Share capital	65,000	
	Retained earnings		10,000
	Bank		55,000
	(for the repurchase of 20,000 shares at $2.75 per share)		

QUESTIONS AND TASKS

1 *Ohope Machinery Limited* has 150,000 shares on issue. These shares had all been issued at a price of $4.00 per share. On 30 June 2017, the company repurchased 25,000 shares at a price of $4.00 per share.

a Prepare the general journal entry to record the repurchase of the shares.

Ohope Machinery Limited
General Journal

b Prepare the equity section and **related notes** of the statement of financial position after the repurchase.

Ohope Machinery Limited
Statement of Financial Position (extract) as at 30 June 2017

Equity	Note	$NZ
Share capital		

Notes to the Statement of Financial Position

_____

_____

2 *Great Dezigns Limited* has issued 750,000 shares at an average price of $1.10 per share. On 31 July 2019, the company repurchased 100,000 shares at $1.20 each. Retained earnings amounted to $240,000 before the repurchase.

a Prepare the general journal entry to record the repurchase of the shares.

Great Dezigns Limited
General Journal

b Prepare the equity section and **related notes** of the statement of financial position after the repurchase.

Great Dezigns Limited
Statement of Financial Position (extract) as at 31 July 2019

Equity	Note	$NZ	$NZ
Share capital			
Retained earnings			
Total equity			

Notes to the Statement of Financial Position

_____

_____

_____

3 *Kilbernie Corporation Limited* has issued shares as follows: 1 million at $1.50 per share, 1.5 million at $2.00 per share and 1.4 million at $1.80 per share. On 31 October 2017 the company repurchased 350,000 shares at $1.90 each. Retained earnings before the repurchase amounted to $1.2 million.

a Calculate the weighted average issue price of the shares.

ANSWER: Weighted average issue price = $ _____

> **REMEMBER!**
>
> The **share capital** repurchased is equal to
>
> Number of shares * weighted average issue price

b Prepare the general journal entry to record the repurchase of the shares.

Kilbernie Corporation Limited
General Journal

c Prepare the equity section and **related notes** of the statement of financial position after the repurchase.

Kilbernie Corporation Limited
Statement of Financial Position (extract) as at 31 October 2017

Equity	Note	$NZ	$NZ
Share capital			
Retained earnings			
Total equity			

Notes to the Statement of Financial Position

_____

_____

4 *Titan Packaging Limited* has issued shares as follows: 300,000 at 75 cents per share, 200,000 at 80 cents per share and 400,000 at 95 cents per share. On 31 May 2015, the company repurchased 400,000 shares at 70 cents per share. Prior to the repurchase, retained earnings amounted to $240,000.

a Calculate the weighted average issue price of the shares

ANSWER: Weighted average issue price = $ _____

4 b   Prepare the journal entry to record the repurchase of the shares.

Titan Packaging Limited
General Journal

c   Prepare the equity section with **related notes** of the statement of financial position after the repurchase.

Titan Packaging Limited
Statement of Financial Position (extract) as at 31 May 2015

Equity	Note	$NZ	$NZ
Share capital			
Retained earnings			
Total equity			

Notes to the Statement of Financial Position

_____

_____

5   *Albany Developments Limited* had issued a total of 500,000 shares at 31 March 2020. Of these, 200,000 had been issued at $2.50 each when the company was first incorporated on 1 July 2017. There had been two subsequent share issues of 150,000 shares: on 1 April 2018 150,000 shares were sold for $3.00 each and on 1 July 2019 150,000 shares were sold for $4.50 each. On 1 May 2020 the company repurchased 50,000 shares.

a   Calculate the weighted average issue price of the shares.

ANSWER: Weighted average issue price = $ _____

b   i   Prepare the journal entry (without narration) to record the repurchase of the shares if the company paid $4.00 per share.

General Journal

ii   Prepare the journal entry (without narration) to record the repurchase of the shares if the company paid $3.00 per share.

General Journal

Revaluation of Property, Plant and Equipment

For some assets, historical cost is not always the most appropriate measurement base because it may not be relevant. For example, the historical cost of land and/or buildings is often well below their current market price. Thus the recoverable amount from land and buildings may be *more* than its historical cost. By continuing to measure such assets at historical cost, the assets of the firm (and hence the equity) are understated and a false measure of financial position is obtained in current terms.

In *The Conceptual Framework* we examined the current cost system of measuring non-current assets where the current value is materially different from the historical cost. The most common assets to be revalued are land and buildings, since these assets often comprise a significant proportion of the total assets of a firm. They are also held for longer than other types of assets, which means that there is more likely to be a material difference between their current value and their historical cost.

> **REMEMBER!**
> Revaluations must be carried out by an **independent registered valuer**.

Example 4

(Ignore GST.) A building had a historical cost of $200,000 and accumulated depreciation of $8,000 at the end of the reporting period, 31 March 2016. After the depreciation entries for the year had been posted, it was revalued by an independent registered valuer at $250,000. Current cost is used to measure land and buildings. Depreciation is charged at 2% per annum. The company's separate income statement showed tax-paid profit for the year of $100,000.

Two journal entries are required:

i **Close the accumulated depreciation account against the asset account**

General Journal

Date	Particulars	Dr $	Cr $
2016 Mar 31	Accumulated depreciation – Building	8,000	
	Building		8,000
	(to close accumulated depreciation on building prior to revaluation)		

ii **Record the revaluation of the building by creating a revaluation surplus**

General Journal

Date	Particulars	Dr $	Cr $
2016 Mar 31	Building	58,000	
	Building revaluation surplus		58,000
	(to record revaluation of building)		

The building revaluation surplus forms part of equity. Movements in the surplus are shown in the statement of comprehensive income:

Statement of Comprehensive Income (extract)[8] for the year ended 31 March 2016

	$NZ
Profit for the year	100,000
Other comprehensive income:	
Gains on property revaluation	58,000
TOTAL COMPREHENSIVE INCOME FOR THE YEAR	$158,000

> **REMEMBER!**
> Income is increases in economic benefits during the accounting period in the form of inflows or enhancements of assets or decreases of liabilities that result in increases in equity, other than those relating to contributions from equity participants.

You should note that the increase in the revaluation surplus **is** a form of **income**, even though it is not shown in the income statement. The revaluation represents an *enhancement* of an asset, in accordance with the definition of income from the *NZ Framework*. However *NZ IAS 16 (39)* prescribes that the increase in the carrying amount is credited directly to equity (and hence does not appear in a separate income statement, but in the statement of comprehensive income).

---

8   For simplicity, this example assumes that the income statement and statement of comprehensive income are prepared as two separate statements.

The increase in the revaluation surplus also appears in the statement of changes in equity, where a separate column for the building revaluation surplus is used.

Statement of Changes in Equity for the year ended 31 March 2016

	Share capital	Retained earnings	Revaluation surplus	Total equity
	$NZ000	*$NZ000*	*$NZ000*	*$NZ000*
Balance at 1 April 2015	....	....	—	....
Changes in equity for 2016				
Issue of share capital	....			....
Dividends		....		....
Total comprehensive income for the year		100	58	158
Balance at 31 March 2016	....	....	58	....

The building revaluation surplus is shown in the equity section of the statement of financial position:

Statement of Financial Position (extract) as at ....

Equity	$NZ
Share capital	
Retained earnings	
Building revaluation surplus	....
	58,000
Total equity	$...........

The depreciation expense for the year was based on the historical amount of $200,000 because the revaluation was carried out at the end of the reporting period. When depreciating revalued assets, the depreciation expense is based on the previous balance up to the date of the revaluation and on the revalued amount thereafter.

Example 5

The building in Example 4 above was located in a thriving provincial town. Some time later, a large industrial centre had been constructed in the town and the values of all property had increased significantly. The building was revalued by an independent registered valuer to its current market value of $400,000 on 30 September 2018. The company's tax-paid profit for the year to 31 March 2019 was $150,000.

When the building is revalued, depreciation is charged on the basis of the previous value up to the date of the revaluation. Depreciation for the years ended 31 March 2017 and 2018 had been based on 2% of the revalued amount of $250,000, or $5,000 per annum. The depreciation for the six months to 30 September 2019 is therefore $^6/_{12}*\$5,000 = \$2,500$.

i   Record the depreciation up to the date of the revaluation

General Journal

Date	Particulars	Dr $	Cr $
2018 Sep 30	Depreciation on building	2,500	
	Accumulated depreciation – Building		2,500
	(to record depreciation on building prior to revaluation)		

ii   Close the accumulated depreciation account against the asset account

General Journal

Date	Particulars	Dr $	Cr $
2018 Sep 30	Accumulated Depreciation – Building	12,500	
	Building		12,500
	(to close accumulated depreciation on building prior to revaluation)		

REMEMBER!

Depreciation on revalued assets is based on the **revalued** amount.

ii Record the revaluation of the building by increasing the revaluation surplus

General Journal

Date	Particulars	Dr $	Cr $
2018 Sep 30	Building Building revaluation surplus (to record revaluation of building)	162,500	162,500

The revaluation is shown in the statement of comprehensive income and statement of changes in equity as follows:

Statement of Comprehensive Income (extract) for the year ended 31 March 2019

	$NZ
Profit for the year	150,000
Other comprehensive income:	
Gains on property revaluation	162,500
TOTAL COMPREHENSIVE INCOME FOR THE YEAR	$312,500

Statement of Changes in Equity for the year ended 31 March 2019

	Share capital	Retained earnings	Revaluation surplus	Total equity
	$NZ000	$NZ000	$NZ000	$NZ000
Balance at 1 April 2018	....	....	58	....
Changes in equity for 2019				
Issue of share capital	....			....
Dividends		....		....
Total comprehensive income for the year		150	162.5	312.5
Balance at 31 March 2019	....	....	220.5	....

The depreciation expense for the remainder of the year is based on the *revalued* amount of $400,000. Using a rate of 2% straight line, the depreciation expense for the remaining six months to 31 March 2019 would be $6/12*2%*\$400,000 = \$4,000$.

The relevant accounts would appear in the general ledger as follows:

General Ledger

Depreciation on Building   7030

Date	Particulars	Dr $	Cr $	Balance $	
2018 Sep 30 2019	Accumulated depreciation – Building	2,500		2,500	Dr
Mar 31	Accumulated depreciation – Building Income summary	4,000	6,500	6,500 —	Dr

Building   2020

Date	Particulars	Dr $	Cr $	Balance $	
2018 Apr 1 Sep 30	Balance Accumulated depreciation – Building Building revaluation surplus	162,500	12,500	250,000 237,500 400,000	Dr Dr Dr

Accumulated Depreciation – Building   2021

Date	Particulars	Dr $	Cr $	Balance $	
2018 Apr 1 Sep 30	Balance Depreciation on building Building	12,500	2,500	10,000 12,500 —	Cr Cr
2019 Mar 31	Depreciation on building		4,000	4,000	Cr

Building Revaluation Surplus				5030	
Date	Particulars	Dr $	Cr $	Balance $	
2018 Apr 1	Balance			58,000	Cr
Sep 30	Building		162,500	220,500	Cr

The carrying amount of the building is now $396,000 ($400,000 – 4,000) and the revised balance of the building revaluation surplus is shown in the equity section of the statement of financial position as before.

Revaluation of Investments

There is a wide variety of investment assets that may be held by companies. In this course we will restrict our coverage to investments in either fixed interest investments, such as government bonds or debentures from other companies, and shares in other companies.

Investments are classified into two groups: available-for sale investments and investments held for trading. The classification of investments in these two groups depends upon management's intent when the investment was purchased.

REMEMBER!

- Available-for-sale investments are **non-current** assets.

- Investments held for trading are **current** assets.

- **Available-for-sale investments** are those investments which management intends to keep in the near term, but nevertheless can be sold at any time. To be classed in this category, management must not have bought them with the intention of actively trading them in the near term. On the other hand, where the investment has a maturity date, such as debentures, management must not have resolved to hold the investments until they mature. (In this latter case, the investment would be classified as a **held-to-maturity investment** which has a different accounting treatment that is beyond the scope of this course.) A company would normally buy available-for-sale investments with the intention of deriving dividend income from the investment. Available-for-sale investments are **non-current** assets.

- **Investments held for trading** are those that the company buys with the *intention* of resale in the near term. Such a company would be actively trading in the sharemarket, with the intention of making profits from increases in the market value of the shares. Investments held for trading are **current assets**.

Measuring Investments

When investments are purchased, *NZ IAS 39* requires that they must be measured at **fair value**. In this course, fair value will normally be historical cost. For available-for-sale investments, fair value also includes any transaction costs associated with the purchase, such as brokerage paid to a sharebroker when buying shares on the New Zealand Exchange.

After the initial purchase, investments are also shown at their fair values, which will (for the purposes of this course) be the value in the marketplace. Accounting entries to record the changes in the value of investments depends on the purpose for which they were originally purchased.

1 Available-for-sale investments
Accounting for available-for sale investments is similar to accounting for property, plant and equipment. A change in value is recorded in a **fair value surplus** account (similar to a land revaluation surplus account).

Example 6

A company purchased 100,000 debentures at $5.00 each on 1 April 2017. Brokerage of 1% was paid at the time of purchase. The debentures are traded in the sharemarket and their market value at 31 March 2018 was $5.20 each. After-tax profit before revaluations was $200,000.

The journal entry to record the purchase of the debentures is:

General Journal

Date	Particulars	Dr $	Cr $
2017 Apr 1	Debentures Bank *(to record purchase of 100,000 debentures at $5.00 each plus 1% brokerage costs)*	505,000	505,000

At 31 March 2014, the debentures have a fair value (as determined by the market) of 100,000 * $5.20 = $520,000. This represents an increase of $520,000 − 505,000 = $15,000 over their historical cost, which was the fair value at the time of purchase.

The journal entry to record the new fair value of the debentures is:

General Journal

Date	Particulars	Dr $	Cr $
2018 Mar 31	Debentures Fair value surplus *(to record revaluation of available-for- sale debentures)*	15,000	15,000

This treatment is the same as for the revaluation of property, plant and equipment. The fair value surplus forms part of comprehensive income, which in turn forms part of equity. Movements in the surplus are shown in the statement of comprehensive income as follows:

Statement of Comprehensive Income (extract) for the year ended 31 March 2018

	$NZ000
Profit for the year	200
Other comprehensive income:	
Available-for-sale financial assets	15
TOTAL COMPREHENSIVE INCOME FOR THE YEAR	$215

The movement in the fair value surplus is also shown in the statement of changes in equity, using a separate column.

Statement of Changes in Equity for the year ended 31 March 2018

	Share capital	Retained earnings	Available-for-sale financial assets	Total equity
	$NZ000	$NZ000	$NZ000	$NZ000
Balance at 1 April 2017	....	....	—	....
Changes in equity for 2018				
Issue of share capital	....			....
Dividends		....		....
Total comprehensive income for the year		200	15	215
Balance at 31 March 2018	....	....	15	....

As with revaluation surpluses for property, plant and equipment, the increase in the fair value surplus is a form of **income**, even though it is not shown in the separate income statement. It forms part of *comprehensive income*. The revaluation represents an *enhancement* of an asset, in accordance with the definition of income from the *NZ Framework*. However *NZ IAS 39 (55)* prescribes that the increase in the gain or loss resulting from the change in fair value of an available-for-sale investment is recognised directly in equity (and hence does not appear in the income statement).

The fair value surplus is shown in the equity section of the statement of financial position:

Statement of Financial Position (extract) as at 31 March 2018

Equity	$NZ
Share capital	....
Retained earnings	....
Fair value surplus	15,000
Total equity	$...........

If the market value of the investment falls below the recorded fair value in a later accounting period, then the decrease in fair value is charged *against* the fair value surplus.

Example 7

Suppose that the fair value of the debentures in Example 6 above at 31 March 2019 was $5.10 each. After-tax paid profit before revaluations was $180,000.

The fair value of the debentures has **decreased** by $520,000 – 510,000 = $10,000. The journal entry to record the loss on change in fair value is:

General Journal

Date	Particulars	Dr $	Cr $
2019 Mar 31	Fair value surplus	10,000	
	Debentures		10,000
	(to record revaluation of available-for-sale debentures)		

The disclosures in the statement of comprehensive income and statement of changes in equity are as follows:

Statement of Comprehensive Income (extract) for the year ended 31 March 2019

	$NZ000
Profit for the year	180
Other comprehensive income:	
Available-for-sale financial assets	(10)
TOTAL COMPREHENSIVE INCOME FOR THE YEAR	$170

Statement of Changes in Equity for the year ended 31 March 2019

	Share capital	Retained earnings	Available-for-sale financial assets	Total equity
	$NZ000	$NZ000	$NZ000	$NZ000
Balance at 1 April 2018	....	....	15	....
Changes in equity for 2019				
Issue of share capital	....			....
Dividends		....		....
Total comprehensive income for the year		180	(10)	170
Balance at 31 March 2019	....	....	5	....

The relevant disclosure in the equity section of the statement of financial position is

Statement of Financial Position (extract) as at 31 March 2019

Equity	$NZ
Share capital	....
Retained earnings	....
Fair value surplus	5,000
Total equity	$...........

The general ledger accounts for debentures and the fair value surplus over the two-year period would appear as follows:

General Ledger

Debentures   2110

Date	Particulars	Dr $	Cr $	Balance $
2017 Apr 1	Bank			505,000 Dr
2018 Mar 31	Fair value surplus	15,000		520,000 Dr
2019 Mar 31	Fair value surplus		10,000	510,000 Dr

Fair Value Surplus   5050

Date	Particulars	Dr $	Cr $	Balance $
2018 Mar 31	Debentures		15,000	15,000 Cr
2019 Mar 31	Debentures	10,000		5,000 Cr

If the fair value of the investment falls below its original cost, then the fair value surplus will have a debit balance. Under some circumstances, this debit balance would be transferred to expenses. However, the circumstances for this to occur are very specific and are beyond the scope of this course.

2   Investments held for trading

Investments held for trading are short-term in nature because the company is buying and selling on a regular basis. *NZ IAS 39* requires that these investments are also recorded at fair value in the financial statements.

The initial fair value of these investments is usually historical cost. Transaction costs are **not** included since the investments are being held in the short term only and the costs of acquiring them are thus treated as expenses when they are incurred.

At the end of the reporting period, these investments are measured at fair value. For equity securities (shares in other companies), this will normally be the closing share price at the end of the reporting period. Any gain or loss of fair value is shown in the income statement.

Example 8

A company purchased 200,000 shares in Telecom at $5.00 each on 1 February 2015. Brokerage of 1% was paid at the time of purchase. The closing price on the New Zealand Exchange at 31 March 2015 was $4.75 each.

The journal entry to record the purchase of the shares is:

General Journal

Date	Particulars	Dr $	Cr $
2015 Feb 1	Shares in Telecom Brokerage expense 　　Bank *(to record purchase of 200,000 shares in Telecom at $5.00 each)*	1,000,000 10,000	1,010,000

At 31 March 2015, the shares have a fair value (as determined by the market) of 200,000 * $4.75 = $950,000. This represents a decrease of $1,000,000 – 950,000 = $50,000 from their historical cost, which was the fair value at the time of purchase.

The journal entry to record the new fair value of the shares is:

General Journal

Date	Particulars	Dr $	Cr $
2015 Mar 31	Loss on revaluation of investments	50,000	
	Shares in Telecom		50,000
	(to record revaluation of Telecom shares held for trading)		

These items would be disclosed in the financial statements as follows:

Statement of Comprehensive Income (extract) $
Administrative expenses
Loss on revaluation of investments held for trading   50,000

Statement of Financial Position (extract) $
Current assets
Investments held for trading   950,000

Note

The loss on revaluation appears as an expense in the statement of comprehensive income (or separate income statement, where prepared. It thus forms part of the profit for the period and is included in the retained earnings column of the statement of changes in equity.

Suppose that the closing share price on 31 March 2015 had been $6.00. The journal entry and financial statement extracts would then be:

General Journal

Date	Particulars	Dr $	Cr $
2015 Mar 31	Shares in Telecom	100,000	
	Gain on revaluation of investments		100,000
	(to record revaluation of Telecom shares held for trading)		

Statement of Comprehensive Income (extract) $
Other income
Gain on revaluation of investments held for trading   100,000

Statement of Financial Position (extract) $
Current assets
Investments held for trading   1,100,000

Summary of Entries for Revaluation of Investments

Type of investment	Comprehensive income	Changes in equity	Financial position
Available-for-sale	Revaluations reported as *Other comprehensive income*	Shown in separate column *Available-for-sale investments*	Shown as *Non-current assets*
Held for trading	Losses reported as *expenses*; gains reported as *Other income*	Included in comprehensive income in *Retained earnings* column	Shown as *Current assets*

QUESTIONS AND TASKS

1 On 31 March 2016 land that had cost $100,000 (excluding GST) was revalued to $120,000.

Prepare the journal entry to record the revaluation of the land.

General Journal

2 A building was purchased on 1 April 2013 for $500,000 (excluding GST). On 31 March 2016, it was revalued by an independent registered valuer to $600,000. Depreciation had been charged at the rate of 2% straight line per annum.

Prepare the journal entries to record the revaluation of the building.

General Journal

3 Machinery that had been purchased for $50,000 (excluding GST) on 1 April 2015 was independently revalued to $75,000 on 31 March 2019, when accumulated depreciation on the machinery was $20,000.

Prepare the journal entries to record the revaluation of the machinery.

General Journal

4 A building was purchased on 1 April 2010 for $200,000 cash (excluding GST). Straight line depreciation was charged at the rate of 2% per annum. On 31 March 2013 the building was independently revalued to its replacement cost of $250,000. During the next few years property prices rose very rapidly and at 31 March 2016 the building was revalued at $450,000

a **i** Prepare the general journal entry to record the revaluation of the building at 31 March 2013.

General Journal

ii Prepare the general journal entry to record the depreciation on the building for the year to 31 March 2016.

General Journal

iii Prepare the general journal entry to record the revaluation of the building at 31 March 2016.

General Journal

b Prepare the ledger accounts below for the period 1 April 2010 to 1 April 2016

General Ledger
Building

Building Revaluation Surplus

5 **Ignore GST in this question.**

Fabulous Fertiliser Limited purchased a specialised item of plant on 1 April 2013 for $300,000 cash. The machine had an estimated useful economic life of six years and residual value of $60,000. The company uses straight line depreciation for all its plant and its reporting period ends on 31 March. On 30 September 2015 the plant was revalued to $360,000. Its estimated life was unchanged but the residual value was revised to $80,000.

a Prepare **all necessary** general journal entries (without narrations) related to the revaluation of the plant.

Fabulous Fertiliser Limited
General Journal

b Prepare the ledger accounts below.

Fabulous Fertiliser Limited
General Ledger

Plant

Plant Revaluation Surplus

c Prepare an extract to show how plant would appear in the **notes** to the statement of financial position prepared at 31 March 2016.

Fabulous Fertiliser Limited
Statement of Financial Position (extract) as at 31 March 2016

Notes to the Statement of Financial Position	

6 On 1 April 2015 debentures were purchased at a cost of $100,000. Brokerage was charged at 1% of the transaction cost. These debentures were intended to be held for the medium term and on 31 March 2016 had a fair value of $102,000.

6 **a** Prepare the journal entry to record the fair value of the debentures at 31 March 2016.

General Journal

b Explain why the debentures are a **non-current** asset.

_____

_____

_____

_____

_____

7 *Share Trading Limited* purchased shares in *Waste Management Limited* on the stock exchange on 1 November 2018 for a total of $35,000. Brokerage costs were an additional 2% of the transaction cost. At the end of the reporting period, 31 December, the shares had a quoted market price of $38,000. The management of *Share Trading Limited* hoped to make a profit by selling these shares early in the new year.

a Prepare the journal entries to record

- the purchase of the shares in *Waste Management Limited*
- the fair value of the shares at 31 December 2018.

Share Trading Limited
General Journal

b Explain why the shares in *Waste Management Limited* are shown as a **current** asset in the statement of financial position of *Share Trading Limited*.

_____

_____

_____

_____

_____

8 On 1 August 2014, *Investor Plan Limited* purchased the following investments:

- 20,000 shares in *The Warehouse Limited* at $4.75 each
- ten-year Government bonds at a total cost of $100,000.

Brokerage costs paid were an additional 2% of the transaction cost.

Investor Plan Limited intended to sell the shares in *The Warehouse Limited* as soon as the share price rose by 10%. However, it was intended to hold the Government bonds until market interest rates fell by at least 2%, which was not expected to occur in the near future.

At the end of the reporting period, 31 March 2015, the market price of the shares was $4.95 each and the quoted price for the government bonds was $105,000.

a Prepare the journal entries to record

- the purchase of the above investments; and
- the fair value of the investments at 31 March 2015.

Investor Plan Limited
General Journal

b Prepare extracts from the financial statements to show how this information would appear at 31 March 2015.

Statement of Financial Position (extract) as at 31 March 2015

Statement of Comprehensive Income (extract) for the year ended 31 March 2015

Statement of Changes in Equity (extract) for the year ended 31 March 2015

	Retained earnings $NZ
Changes in equity for 2015	

9 The accounts below have been extracted from the general ledger of *Up-to-Date Investments Limited* at 31 March 2016.

Debentures

Date	Particulars	Dr $	Cr $	Balance	
2016 Mar 31	Balance			200,000	Dr
	Fair value surplus	20,000		220,000	Dr

Fair Value Surplus

Date	Particulars	Dr $	Cr $	Balance	
2016 Mar 31	Balance			50,000	Cr
	Debentures		20,000	70,000	Cr

Shares in Contact Energy

Date	Particulars	Dr $	Cr $	Balance	
2016 Mar 31	Balance			100,000	Dr
	Gain on revaluation	37,000		137,000	Dr

Gain on Revaluation

Date	Particulars	Dr $	Cr $	Balance	
2016 Mar 31	Balance			—	
	Shares in Contact Energy		37,000	37,000	Cr
	Income summary	37,000		—	

a   i **Fully describe** the events/s that gave rise to the entry in the **fair value surplus** account.

_____

_____

_____

_____

_____

ii **Fully describe** the events/s that gave rise to the entry in the **Shares in Contact Energy** account.

_____

_____

_____

_____

_____

b **Fully explain the purpose** of the entries in the **gain on revaluation** account.

_____

_____

_____

_____

_____

c Prepare extracts from the statement of financial position to show how the **assets** would be disclosed at 31 March 2016.

_____

_____

_____

_____

_____

_____

Distributions of Shares

A distribution of shares may be made by a company to existing shareholders. This is commonly known as a **share split**. The additional shares are issued in proportion to the number of shares already held, so that the proportion of the company owned by any particular shareholder after the issue is the same as before.

For example, a company has 500,000 issued shares and makes a 1 for 10 distribution. This means that shareholders receive one additional share for every ten shares currently held.

Consider of A Smith who owns 10,000 shares in the company before the new issue:

	Before new issue	After new issue
Total number of shares issued	500,000	550,000
Number owned by A Smith	10,000	11,000
Proportion of company owned by A Smith	2.0%	2.0%

A Smith owns 2.0% of the company shares both before and after the share split. If the company continues to pay the same rate of dividend per share as before, however, then A Smith would receive a higher dividend payout after the share split than before.

The market may perceive a distribution of shares or share split as an intention by the company to increase the overall level of dividend payments. From this, the market may perceive that the company expects an increase in its profitability.

A distribution of shares or share split does not alter the dollar value of share capital and therefore does not require a journal entry. The increase in the number of shares on issue is recorded in the notes to the statement of financial position.

Distributions of shares from other equity accounts

Sometimes distributions of shares are made from either an asset revaluation surplus or retained earnings. These are simply a transfer from either of these equity accounts to share capital. The amount transferred to share capital for each share must be the fair value of the share.

Example 9

A company with 1 million shares on issue made a distribution from the land revaluation surplus of 1 share for every 20 held. The market price of the shares is $2.00.

The number of shares issued is 1,000,000 / 20 = 50,000. Each share has a fair value of $2.00, thus the total increase in share capital = 50,000 * $2.00 = $100,000.

The journal entry to record the distribution is as follows:

General Journal

Date	Particulars	Dr $	Cr $
	Land revaluation surplus	100,000	
	Share capital		100,000
	(to record a distribution of 1 share for 20 at a value of $2.00 per share from the land revaluation surplus)		

If the distribution had been made from retained earnings, the journal entry would be:

General Journal

Date	Particulars	Dr $	Cr $
	Retained earnings	100,000	
	Share capital		100,000
	(to record a distribution of 1 share for 20 at a value of $2.00 per share from retained earnings)		

Disclosure
- There has been no change on the total equity of the company as a result of the distribution, but the classes of equity have changed. In the statement of changes in equity, share capital shows an increase and the source account shows a decrease on the same line.
- There has been a movement in both share capital and the source account. These changes would be disclosed in the notes to the statement of financial position.

QUESTIONS AND TASKS

---

1 *Middlemore Limited* made a distribution of 50,000 shares on 31 July 2016 from its land revaluation surplus. The shares had a fair value of $2.00 each.

Prepare the journal entry to record the distribution of shares.

Middlemore Limited
General Journal

---

2 *Ngaiotonga Investments Limited* had share capital of $500,000 (1,000,000 shares) at 30 June 2014. The company made a distribution from retained earnings of one share for every ten held on that date, when the fair value of the company's shares was 60 cents.

Prepare the journal entry to record the distribution of shares.

Ngaiotonga Investments Limited
General Journal

---

3 *Ruakaka Holdings Limited* had the following equity balances at 31 August 2017:

Share capital (300,000 shares)	$ 900,000
Retained earnings	450,000
Building revaluation surplus	200,000
	$1,550,000

On 1 September 2017, the company made a distribution of one share for every six held on 31 August. Half of the distribution was from the building revaluation surplus and half from retained earnings. The fair value of the shares issued was $3.20.

a Prepare the journal entry to record the distribution of shares.

Ruakaka Holdings Limited
General Journal

b Prepare the equity section of the statement of financial position with related notes after the distribution of shares on 31 August 2017.

Ruakaka Holdings Limited
Statement of Financial Position (extract) as at 31 August 2017

Equity	Note	$NZ	$NZ
Share capital			
Retained earnings			
Building revaluation surplus			
Total equity			

Notes to the Statement of Financial Position

---

4 *Hikurangi Limited* had the following equity balances at 31 March 2018:

Share capital (100,000 shares)	$250,000
Retained earnings	100,000
Land revaluation surplus	20,000
	$370,000

The following events occurred in the year to 31 March 2019:

- The company made a distribution of shares from retained earnings of one share for every five held on 31 March 2018. The fair value of the shares issued was $2.75.
- The land was revalued from $90,000 to $100,000.
- The tax-paid profit for the year was $65,000.
- A dividend of $15,000 was paid during the year.

a Prepare the retained earnings account.

Retained Earnings

b Prepare the equity section of the statement of financial position with related notes as at 31 March 2019.

Hikurangi Limited
Statement of Financial Position (extract) as at 31 March 2019

Equity	Note	$NZ	$NZ
Share capital			
Retained earnings			
Land revaluation surplus			
Total equity			

Notes to the Statement of Financial Position

The Statement of Changes in Equity – A Summary

The last three chapters have been concerned with all of the transactions that affect the equity of a company. The following transactions have been explained:

- issue of shares in return for cash and/or other assets
- issue of shares in satisfaction of liabilities
- issue of shares in return for taking over a business
- accounting for company income tax
- accounting for dividends paid
- repurchase of shares
- revaluation of non-current assets
- closing entries to income summary.

All of these transactions are shown in the statement of changes in equity.

Disclosure Requirements

NZ IAS 1 (106) requires the following disclosures in the statement of changes in equity:
- total comprehensive income for the period (from the statement of comprehensive income)
- the amounts of transactions with owners in their capacity as owners, showing separately contributions by and distributions to owners (eg share issues, share repurchases, dividends)
- for each component of equity, a reconciliation between the carrying amount at the beginning and the end of the period, separately disclosing each change.

Example 10

Andreas Holdings Limited had total equity of $1,000,000 at 1 April 2018, consisting of share capital of $700,000, retained earnings of $250,000, a land revaluation surplus of $50,000 and a fair value surplus relating to available-for-sale investments of $25,000. During the year ended 31 March 2019, the following events occurred:

- *Land was revalued upwards by $20,000.*
- *The tax-paid profit for the year was $150,000 and a dividend of $40,000 was paid.*
- *New shares with a total value of $250,000 were issued to the public for cash.*
- *40,000 shares which had a weighted average issue price of $2.00 each were repurchased from existing shareholders for $100,000.*
- *The available-for-sale investments were revalued downwards by $5,000.*

The statement of comprehensive income is as follows:

Statement of Comprehensive Income (extract) for the year ended 31 March 2019

	$NZ000
Profit for the year	150
Other comprehensive income:	
Gains on property revaluation	20
Available-for-sale financial assets	(5)
TOTAL COMPREHENSIVE INCOME FOR THE YEAR	$165

The statement of changes in equity for the company is shown below.

Andreas Holdings Limited
Statement of Changes in Equity for the year ended 31 March 2019

	Share capital	Retained earnings	Revaluation surplus	Available-for-sale investments	Total equity
	$NZ000	$NZ000	$NZ000	$NZ000	$NZ000
Balance at 1 April 2018	700	250	50	25	1,025
Changes in equity for 2019					
Issue of share capital	250				250
Repurchase of share capital	(80)	(20)			(100)
Dividends		(40)			(40)
Total comprehensive income for the year		150	20	(5)	165
Balance at 31 March 2019	870	340	70	20	1,300

KEY POINTS

- Companies with excess cash may wish to repurchase their own shares. Such a repurchase *reduces* the share capital of the company.

  - The amount of share capital repurchased is based on the number of shares and the weighted average price that the company has received for all shares currently on issue.

  - If shares are purchased at an amount higher than the weighted average price, then effectively a loss has been made on the repurchase. The amount of the loss is charged to retained earnings:

Dr	Share capital	
Dr	Retained earnings	
Cr		Bank

  - If shares are purchased at an amount that is less than the weighted average price, then effectively a gain has been made on the repurchase. The amount of the gain is credited to retained earnings:

Dr	Share capital	
Cr		Retained earnings
Cr		Bank

  - The repurchase of shares is shown in the statement of changes in equity.

  - Repurchase of shares is subject to the **solvency test**.

- Most companies use **current cost** revaluation model to account for significant assets such as land, buildings and *available-for-sale* investments. The current cost is determined by an independent registered valuer for property assets and the market price for investments.

  - The increase in the value that results when current cost is used is credited to a revaluation surplus which forms part of equity:

Dr	Asset	
Cr		Revaluation/ Fair value surplus

  - Businesses that use the current cost system have some of their assets stated at historical cost and some stated at current cost.

  - Revaluations of non-current assets are shown in the statement of comprehensive income and the statement of changes in equity.

  - The calculation of the depreciation expense for a revalued asset is based on its revalued amount from the date of the revaluation.

- Revaluation of *investments held for trading* are recorded as gains or losses:

Dr	Investment		OR	Dr	Loss on revaluation
Cr	Gain on revaluation			Cr	Investment

- A company may make a distribution of shares. New shares must be issued in proportion to the number of shares already held so that the proportion of a company owned by any single shareholder remains the same after the share split as before. No journal entry is required.

- A company may distribute shares from other equity accounts (commonly retained earnings or an asset revaluation surplus).

  - A distribution converts surpluses to share capital:

Dr	Retained earnings/ Asset revaluation surplus	
Cr		Share capital

  - A distribution must be made using a fair value for the shares.

  - A distribution of shares does not affect total equity. The components of equity are reorganised and shown in the statement of changes in equity.

  - The changes in equity account balances resulting from a distribution of shares are disclosed in the notes to the statement of financial position.

QUESTIONS AND TASKS

a Prepare the statement of comprehensive income for the year ended 31 March 2015.

Handsoff Limited
Statement of Comprehensive Income for the year ended 31 March 2015

	$NZ000
Profit for the year	**250**
Gain on property revaluation	
TOTAL COMPREHENSIVE INCOME FOR THE YEAR	

b Prepare the statement of changes in equity for the year ended 31 March 2015.

Handsoff Limited
Statement of Changes in Equity for the year ended 31 March 2015

	Share capital $NZ000	Retained earnings $NZ000	Revaluation surplus $NZ000	Total equity $NZ000
Balance at 1 April 2014	**300**	**160**	**40**	**500**
Changes in equity for 2015				
Issue of share capital				
Dividends				
Total comprehensive income for the year				
Balance at 31 March 2015				

a Prepare the statement of comprehensive income for the year ended 31 March 2017.

Gastric Delights Limited
Statement of Comprehensive Income for the year ended 31 March 2017

	$NZ000
Profit for the year	**60**
Gain on plant revaluation	
TOTAL COMPREHENSIVE INCOME FOR THE YEAR	

2 continued

b Prepare the statement of changes in equity for the year ended 31 March 2017.

Gastric Delights Limited
Statement of Changes in Equity for the year ended 31 March 2017

	Share capital $NZ000	Retained earnings $NZ000	Revaluation surplus $NZ000	Total equity $NZ000
Balance at 1 April 2016	200	95	40	335
Changes in equity for 2017				
Repurchase of share capital				
Dividends				
Total comprehensive income for the year				
Balance at 31 March 2017				

---

3 *ConnectNet Limited* is an internet service provider. On 1 May 2016 the company had the following equity balances:

Share capital (2,000,000 shares fully paid)	$2,000,000
Retained earnings	400,000
Fair value surplus	30,000

During the year to 30 April 2017, the following events were recorded:

- A final dividend of 6 cents per share was paid on 31 May 2016 for the year ended 30 April 2016. All shareholders as at 1 May 2016 were entitled to this dividend.
- *ConnectNet* issued a further 400,000 shares at $1.20 per share on 30 June 2016.
- An interim dividend of 4 cents per share was paid to all shareholders on 20 September 2016.
- Available-for-sale investments were revalued upward by $30,000 on 30 April 2017.
- The profit after tax for the year to 30 April 2017 was $240,000.

---

a Prepare the statement of comprehensive income for the year ended 30 April 2017.

ConnectNet Limited
Statement of Comprehensive Income for the year ended 30 April 2017

	$NZ000
Profit for the year	240
Available-for-sale financial assets	
TOTAL COMPREHENSIVE INCOME FOR THE YEAR	

b Prepare the statement of changes in equity for the year ended 30 April 2017.

ConnectNet Limited
Statement of Changes in Equity for the year ended 30 April 2017

	Share capital $NZ000	Retained earnings $NZ000	Available-for-sale financial assets $NZ000	Total equity $NZ000
Balance at 1 May 2016	2,000	400	30	2,430
Changes in equity for 2017				
Issue of share capital				
Dividends				
Total comprehensive income for the year				
Balance at 30 April 2017				

3 c Prepare the equity section of the statement of financial position with related notes as at 30 April 2017.

ConnectNet Limited
Statement of Financial Position (extract) as at 30 April 2017

Equity	Note	$NZ	$NZ
Share capital			
Retained earnings			
Fair value surplus			
Total equity			

Notes to the Statement of Financial Position

---

4 *Aero Engineering Services Limited* is an engineering company specialising in repairing small aircraft. The following are the company's equity balances as at 1 July 2018:

Share capital (1,000,000 shares fully paid)	$800,000
Retained earnings	150,000
Land revaluation surplus	50,000

During the year to 30 June 2019, the following events were recorded:

- On 10 August 2018 a final dividend of 5 cents per share was paid to all shareholders holding shares on 1 July 2018. This dividend related to the year ended 30 June 2018.
- An interim dividend of 6 cents per share was paid to all shareholders on 31 December 2018. All shareholders owning shares on this date were entitled to receive the dividend.
- *Aero Engineering Services* bought back from shareholders 100,000 shares at a price of $1.00. These shares had been issued at a weighted average price of 70 cents. This transaction took place on 30 May 2019.
- Land was revalued from $250,000 to $275,000 on 30 June 2019.
- The profit after tax was $180,000 for the year ended 30 June 2019.

a Prepare the journal entry for the repurchase of shares on 30 May 2019.

Aero Engineering Services Limited
General Journal

b Prepare the statement of changes in equity for the year ended 30 June 2019.

Aero Engineering Services Limited
Statement of Changes in Equity for the year ended 30 June 2019

	Share capital $NZ000	Retained earnings $NZ000	Revaluation surplus $NZ000	Total equity $NZ000
Balance at 1 July 2018	800	150	50	1,000
Changes in equity for 2019				
Repurchase of share capital				
Dividends				
Total comprehensive income for the year				
Balance at 30 June 2019				

continued

4 continued

c   Prepare the retained earnings account for the year.

Aero Engineering Services Limited
General Ledger

Retained Earnings

d   Prepare the equity section of the statement of financial position with related notes as at 30 June 2019.

Aero Engineering Services Limited
Statement of Financial Position (extract) as at 30 June 2019

Equity	Note	$NZ	$NZ
Total equity			

Notes to the Statement of Financial Position

---

5   *Budget Earthmoving Contractors Limited* is a firm of contractors that specialises in earthmoving for new housing subdivisions. The company had the following equity balances as at 1 April 2018:

Share capital (75 cent shares)	$900,000
Retained earnings	300,000
Land revaluation surplus	140,000
Fair value surplus	55,000

During the year to 31 March 2019, the following events were recorded:

- On 30 April 2018 a final dividend of 5 cents per share was paid for the previous year. All shareholders holding shares on 31 March 2018 were eligible to receive this dividend.
- *Budget Earthmoving Contractors* issued a further 400,000 shares at 75 cents. This transaction took place on 30 September 2018.
- Available-for-sale investments consisted of shares in *Telecom*, which were revalued downwards by $3,000 at the end of the reporting period.
- On 30 November 2018, an interim dividend of 3 cents per share was paid to all shareholders holding shares on that date.
- An independent valuer revalued the land upwards by $50,000 on 31 March 2019.
- The profit after tax was $132,000 for the year ended 31 March 2019.

a   Prepare the journal entry to record the revaluation of land.

Budget Earthmoving Contractors Limited
General Journal

5 b Prepare the journal entry to record the revaluation of the *Telecom* shares.

Budget Earthmoving Contractors Limited
General Journal

c Prepare the statement of comprehensive income for the year ended 31 March 2019.

Budget Earthmoving Contractors Limited
Statement of Comprehensive Income for the year ended 31 March 2019

	$NZ000
Profit for the year	
TOTAL COMPREHENSIVE INCOME FOR THE YEAR	

d Prepare the statement of changes in equity for the year ended 31 March 2019.

Budget Earthmoving Contractors Limited
Statement of Changes in Equity for the year ended 31 March 2019

	Share capital	Retained earnings	Revaluation surplus	Available-for-sale financial assets	Total equity
	$NZ000	$NZ000	$NZ000	$NZ000	$NZ000
Balance at 1 April 2018	900	300	140	55	1,395
Changes in equity for 2019					
Issue of share capital					
Dividends					
Total comprehensive income for the year					
Balance at 31 March 2019					

e Prepare the equity section of the statement of financial position and related notes as at 31 March 2019.

Budget Earthmoving Contractors Limited
Statement of Financial Position (extract) as at 31 March 2019

Equity	Note	$NZ	$NZ
Total equity			

Notes to the Statement of Financial Position

_____

_____

_____

6 *Dynamic Industries Limited* is owned by three brothers and operates as a wholesaler and distributor of fitness equipment. Below are the company's statements of changes in equity for the years ended 31 December 2016 and 2017.

Additional Information
- The company has a policy of not paying an interim dividend, and pays a final dividend to shareholders on 1 February each year.
- During the year to 31 December 2017 the only shares issued were in exchange for a piece of land.
- Shares issued by the company have a fair value of 50 cents.
- Land owned by the company is valued each year by a registered independent valuer.
- Shares have not been repurchased from shareholders during the periods.

Dynamic Industries Limited
Statement of Changes in Equity for the year ended 31 December 2017

	Share capital	Retained earnings	Land revaluation surplus	Total equity
	$NZ000	$NZ000	$NZ000	$NZ000
Balance at 1 January 2016	550	200	50	800
Changes in equity for 2016				
Dividends		(130)		(130)
Total comprehensive income for the year		150	40	190
Balance at 31 December 2016	**$550**	**$220**	**$90**	**$860**
Balance at 1 January 2017	550	220	90	860
Changes in equity for 2017				
Issue of share capital	100			100
Dividends		(100)		(100)
Total comprehensive income for the year		70	20	90
Balance at 31 December 2017	**$650**	**$190**	**$110**	**$950**

Prepare the general journal entries to explain the events in the statement of changes in equity above for the year ended 31 December 2017.

Dynamic Industries Limited
General Journal

ADDITIONAL QUESTIONS

1 *McCallum Recording and Production* is a small family business, operating as a partnership, that records and produces local music artists. The family has decided to change the ownership structure of the business to a company. The company was incorporated on 1 February 2015 and shares were issued to the three partners on 16 February in exchange for selected assets and liabilities of the partnership. The following were taken over at the amounts shown:

Assets		Liabilities	
Bank	$10,000	Accounts payable	$14,000
Accounts receivable	15,000	Loan (8%, due 31 October 2020)	90,000
Buildings	80,000		
Equipment	60,000		
Land	120,000		

The company was called *McCallum Studios Limited* and consideration given to partners was 500,000 shares with a fair value of 45 cents each.

During the year ended 31 January 2016, the following events occurred:

- An invoice for preliminary expenses of $4,000 (exclusive of GST) was received on 20 February 2015.
- On 31 July 2015 the directors resolved to issue a further 250,000 shares at a price of 60 cents to other family members to fund expansion. These shares were issued on 20 August.
- On 30 November 2015 one of the shareholders made a decision to sell her shares back to the company as she was no longer able to continue working in the business. K McCallum held 40,000 shares; the repurchase price was agreed at 60 cents per share.
- An interim dividend of $26,400 was paid on 31 December 2015.

At the end of the reporting period the following information was provided:

- The following balances were available from the general ledger of *McCallum Studios Limited*:

Bank	$75,100 Dr	Accounts payable	$16,000 Cr
GST	5,100 Dr	Loan (8%, due 31 October 2020)	70,000 Cr
Accounts receivable	20,000 Dr		

- Depreciation is to be charged at 2% for buildings and 20% for equipment, both based on cost and using a monthly depreciation policy. Additional equipment of $120,000 had been purchased on 1 September.
- The land was revalued by an independent valuer on 31 January 2016 to $140,000 due to an upturn in the property market.
- The profit before tax was $94,000.
- Tax of $28,200 is to be paid. No provisional tax has been paid.

a Prepare general journal entries **without narrations** to record the following:

- purchase of the partnership and settlement with the vendors
- formation costs (Remember the GST!)
- the issue of additional shares
- the repurchase of shares (Remember to use the weighted average issue price.)
- the interim dividend paid
- the revaluation of land
- the income tax expense
- closing entries for the income tax expense, income summary and interim dividend accounts.

McCallum Studios Limited
General Journal

McCallum Studios Limited
General Journal (continued)

b Prepare the statement of changes in equity for the year ended 31 January 2016.

McCallum Studios Limited
Statement of Changes in Equity for the year ended 31 January 2016

	Share capital $NZ	Retained earnings $NZ	Revaluation surplus $NZ	Total equity $NZ
Balance at 1 February 2015	—	—	—	—
Changes in equity for 2016				
Issue of share capital				
Repurchase of share capital				
Dividends paid				
Total comprehensive income for the year				
Balance at 31 January 2016				

1 c Prepare the statement of financial position as at 31 January 2016.

McCallum Studios Limited
Statement of Financial Position as at 31 January 2016

2 *J C Cattery Limited* operates a boutique cattery. The following represents a summary of the company's statement of financial position as at 31 December 2015:

J C Cattery Limited
Statement of Financial Position as at 31 December 2015

Assets	$	Liabilities	$
Accounts receivable	5,000	Accounts payable	4,000
Bank	30,000	Loan (8.5%, due 15 May 2025)	110,000
Buildings (cost)	165,000	GST	2,400
Less: Accumulated depreciation	(13,200)	Equity	
Land (valuation)	230,000	200,000 shares fully paid	200,000
Fixtures and fittings (cost)	28,000	Retained earnings	100,000
Less: Accumulated depreciation	(8,400)	Land revaluation surplus	20,000
	$436,400		$436,400

During the year ended 31 December 2016 the following events occurred:

- A final dividend for the year ended 31 December 2015 of $15,000 was paid on 28 February 2016.
- The directors offered existing shareholders the opportunity to purchase additional shares at $1.00 each. One additional share was offered for every 20 held. All shareholders accepted the offer and the shares were issued on 31 July 2016.
- An interim dividend of $7,000 was paid on 30 September 2016.
- The total provisional tax payment for the year was $9,900, paid in two equal instalments on 28 July 2016 and 7 February 2017.

At the end of the reporting period the following information was provided:

- The following balances were available from the general ledger of *J C Cattery Limited*:

Bank	$4,850 Cr	Accounts payable	$6,000 Cr
Accounts receivable	12,000 Dr	GST	2,000 Cr
Government bonds (6%, due 31 Dec 2018)	50,000 Dr	Loan (8.5%, due 15 May 2025)	100,000 Cr

- Depreciation is to be charged on buildings at 2% per annum and for fixtures and fittings at 15% per annum, both based on cost.
- The profit before tax was $40,000, with tax paid at 30%.
- Land was revalued to independent valuation of $300,000 at the end of the reporting period.
- The government bonds were purchased to provide interest income for the company in the medium term.

a Prepare general journal entries to record the following to **31 December 2016**:

- payment of provisional tax
- the issue of shares
- payment of the final and interim dividends
- the revaluation of land
- the income tax expense.

J C Cattery Limited
General Journal

J C Cattery Limited
General Journal (continued)

b Prepare the statement of changes in equity for the year ended 31 December 2016.

J C Cattery Limited
Statement of Changes in Equity for the year ended 31 December 2016

	Share capital	Retained earnings	Revaluation surplus	Total equity
	$NZ	$NZ	$NZ	$NZ
Balance at 1 January 2016	200,000	100,000	20,000	320,000
Changes in equity for 2016				
Issue of share capital				
Dividends				
Total comprehensive income for the year				
Balance at 31 December 2016				

c Prepare the statement of financial position as at 31 December 2016.

J C Cattery Limited
Statement of Financial Position as at 31 December 2016

continued

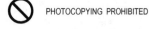

J C Cattery Limited
Statement of Financial Position (continued) as at 31 December 2016

3 *Superior Medical Equipment Limited* is a firm supplying specialised medical equipment to hospitals. The following equity balances have been extracted from the ledger as at 31 March 2018, after all closing entries had been prepared and posted for the year:

Share capital (200,000 shares)	$400,000 Cr
Land revaluation surplus	150,000 Cr
Retained earnings	100,000 Cr

A note in the Annual Report for the year disclosed a proposed final dividend of $40,000 for the year.

During the year ended 31 March 2019 the following events occurred:

- An offer of shares was made to existing shareholders to purchase additional shares for $2.50 each. Shareholders were entitled to one additional share for every eight shares held. All shareholders accepted the offer and the shares were issued on 15 April 2018.
- A prospectus was issued on 1 May 2018 inviting the public to apply for 200,000 shares at a price of $2.50 per share, payable in full upon application. The issue closed on 31 May by which time applications had been received for 300,000 shares. Of these, applications for 50,000 were rejected outright and returned with the cheques to applicants. The remainder of the cheques were banked, with the applications being scaled down on a pro-rata basis. The shares were allotted on 15 June and the refund cheques were posted to the applicants the same day.
- The proposed final dividend for the 2018 financial year was paid on 15 July.
- An interim dividend of 5 cents per share was paid to all shareholders on 31 October 2018. All shareholders were entitled to participate in the dividend.
- An independent valuer revalued the land upwards by $50,000 on 31 March 2019.
- The profit after tax for the year was $120,000 for the year ended 31 March 2019.
- A final dividend of 8 cents per share was proposed by the directors of the company on 15 May 2019.

3 **a** Prepare the journal entries, including closing entries, to record the above events. Narrations are **not** required.

Superior Medical Equipment Limited
General Journal

b Prepare a note disclosing the proposed final dividend for the 2019 year.

_____

_____

_____

_____

3 continued

c Explain why the **proposed final dividend** is shown as a note to the financial statements and is not shown in the statement of financial position.

_____

_____

_____

_____

d Prepare the statement of changes in equity for the year ended 31 March 2019.

Superior Medical Equipment Limited
Statement of Changes in Equity for the year ended 31 March 2019

	Share capital $NZ	Retained earnings $NZ	Revaluation surplus $NZ	Total equity $NZ
Balance at 1 April 2018	**400,000**	**100,000**	**150,000**	**650,000**
Changes in equity for 2019				
Issue of share capital				
Dividends				
Total comprehensive income for the year				
Balance at 31 March 2019				

e Prepare the equity section, including related **notes**, of the statement of financial position as at 31 March 2019.

Superior Medical Equipment Limited
Statement of Financial Position (extract) as at 31 March 2019

Equity			

Notes to the Statement of Financial Position

_____

_____

_____

f Explain why an **independent** valuer was used to revalue the land.

_____

_____

_____

_____

_____

g Explain why the increase in land value forms part of **income**.

_____

_____

_____

_____

_____

REVISION QUESTIONS

1 Kupe and Maui have been in partnership as fishermen for many years. Their current accounts prepared at 31 March 2016 are shown below. Study the accounts and answer the questions that follow.

Kupe – Current Account

Date	Particulars	Debit	Credit	Balance	
2016	Balance			30,000	Cr
Mar 31	Interest on capital		12,000	42,000	Cr
	Salary		25,000	67,000	Cr
	Share of residue		43,500	110,500	Cr
	Interest on loan		1,500	112,000	Cr
	Interest on drawings	900		111,100	Cr
	Kupe – Drawings	36,000		75,100	Cr

Maui – Current Account

Date	Particulars	Debit	Credit	Balance	
2016	Balance			20,000	Cr
Mar 31	Interest on capital		8,000	28,000	Cr
	Salary		40,000	68,000	Cr
	Share of residue		21,750	89,750	Cr
	Interest on drawings	1,200		88,550	Cr
	Maui – Drawings	48,000		40,550	Cr

Additional information:
- Kupe made a short-term loan to the partnership on 1 April 2015 at an interest rate of 5% per annum. The loan will be repaid in two years' time.
- Interest on drawings is charged on the average balance throughout the year.
- Interest on capital is payable at 8% per annum on the average capital balance. Both partners contributed $30,000 additional capital on 1 October 2015.

a Calculate the amount of Kupe's loan to the partnership.

_____

_____

_____

_____

_____

b Prepare the journal entry (without narration) to record the interest expense on Kupe's loan.

General Journal

c Calculate the **interest rate** payable on drawings.

_____

_____

_____

_____

_____

_____

d Prepare the journal entry (without narration) to close Maui's Drawings account.

General Journal

e Calculate the profit of the partnership before any distribution was made.

_____

_____

_____

_____

f Calculate the balance of **Kupe's capital** account at 31 March 2016.

_____

_____

_____

_____

g Calculate the balance of **Maui's capital** account at 31 March 2016.

_____

_____

_____

_____

h What is the ratio in which residual profits are shared between the partners?

Kupe [:   ] Maui

i Prepare the journal entry (without narration) to allocate the residue to the partners.

General Journal

j On 1 April 2016, the partners decided to change their profit-sharing arrangement so that they received equal shares. Maui's fixed capital is to be increased so that capital balances are equal, with the transfer being made from his current account.

Prepare the journal entry (without narration) to record this transfer.

General Journal

2   *Plant Kingdom Limited* was registered on 1 April 2015. The company was formed for the purpose of establishing a nation-wide chain of garden centres. On the same day, a prospectus was issued inviting the public to apply for 200,000 shares at $5.00 each, fully payable on application. By the closing date, 1 June 2015, applications had been received for 250,000 shares. Cheques for $50,000 were returned to applicants as their application forms had not been completed correctly. The remaining applications were scaled down and shares were allotted on a pro-rata basis on 30 June 2015, with refund cheques being mailed the same day.

On 1 September 2015, *Plant Kingdom Limited* entered into an agreement to take over various assets and liabilities of *Gladys' Glorious Gardens Limited* for a total consideration of $350,000. A summary of the statement of financial position of *Gladys' Glorious Gardens Limited* as at 31 August 2015 is shown below.

Gladys' Glorious Gardens Limited
Summary Statement of Financial Position as at 31 August 2015

	$000	$000	$000
Assets			
Bank		30	
Accounts receivable		15	
Inventory		70	
Land		200	
Buildings	100		
Less: Accumulated depreciation – Buildings	20		
		80	
Total assets			$395
Liabilities			
GST		3	
Accounts payable		17	
Income tax payable		20	
Mortgage on land and buildings		75	
Total liabilities			115
Equity			280
Total equity and liabilities			$395

The agreement for sale and purchase states that all assets and liabilities will be taken over on 30 September except the bank account, GST and income tax payable. Carrying amounts at 31 August will be used, with the following exceptions:

i   Accounts receivable is to be valued at $12,000 after writing off bad debts of $1,800.
ii   Land is to be valued at government valuation of $250,000.

The owners of *Gladys' Glorious Gardens Limited* are to receive 50,000 shares in *Plant Kingdom Limited* at a fair value of $5.00 each on 30 September, with the balance of the consideration to be paid in cash on 15 October.

Prepare entries in general journal format (including dates, but without narrations) to record

- the public share issue for *Plant Kingdom Limited*
- the acquisition of assets and liabilities of *Gladys' Glorious Gardens Limited*
- settlement with the owners of *Gladys' Glorious Gardens Limited*.

General Journal

General Journal (continued)

---

3 The journal entries below have been extracted from the books of *Krazy Komputers Limited*. Before the year-end entries were prepared, the company had share capital of $450,000, which represented 200,000 shares fully paid, and retained earnings of $140,000. The profit before tax for the year ended 31 March 2017 was $220,000. Company tax is payable at 30%. The fair value of the shares at 31 March 2017 was $2.50.

Krazy Komputers Limited
General Journal

	Date	Particulars	Dr $	Cr $
i	2017 Mar 31	Land	50,000	
		Land revaluation surplus		50,000
ii		Mortgage on land and buildings	100,000	
		Share capital		100,000
iii		Share capital	45,000	
		Bank		42,000
		Retained earnings		3,000
iv		Income tax expense	66,000	
		Income tax payable		66,000

a Write a sentence that *fully describes* the transaction or event represented by **each** of the journal entries above.

i _____

_____

_____

ii _____

_____

_____

iii _____

_____

_____

iv _____

_____

_____

b Prepare the journal entry (without narration) to close the **income summary** account at 31 March 2017.

General Journal

c Prepare the **retained earnings** account for the year to 31 March 2017.

General Ledger

Retained Earnings

d Calculate the *total comprehensive income* that would be shown in the **statement of changes in equity** for the year ended 31 March 2017.

_____

_____

_____

_____

_____

e Calculate the number of shares on issue at 31 March 2017.

_____

_____

_____

f On 20 April 2017, the directors declared a dividend of 5 cents per share for the year to 31 March 2017, to be paid on 31 May.

i Prepare the journal entry (without narration) to record the payment of the dividend.

General Journal

ii Explain how this dividend would be disclosed in the financial statements for the company prepared at 31 March 2017.

_____

_____

_____

g The balance of the **income tax payable** account in the ledger of *Krazy Komputers Limited* at 1 April 2016 was $5,500 Cr. This amount was paid to Inland Revenue on 7 April 2016. The company made one payment of $60,000 for provisional tax on 15 January 2017.

Prepare the **income tax payable** account of *Krazy Komputers Limited* for the year to 31 March 2017.

General Ledger

Income Tax Payable

---

4 On 1 April 2016, the balances of the share capital account and retained earnings account of *Final Choice Limited* were $400,000 Cr and $200,000 Cr respectively. There were 160,000 shares on issue. The company also had a fair value surplus amounting to $50,000 Cr, relating to available-for-sale investments that were valued at $120,000.
The following events occurred in the year to 31 March 2017:

- The final dividend of $20,000 for the year ended 31 March 2016 was paid on 20 May 2016.
- On 30 June 2016, the company repurchased 40,000 shares at a price of $2.60 each.
- An offer had been made to existing shareholders to buy shares on the basis of one new share for every eight shares held. The price of the shares was $2.75. All shareholders accepted the offer and the shares were issued on 30 September 2016.
- An interim dividend of $15,000 for the year to 31 March 2017 was paid on 20 November 2016.
- Available-for-sale investments were revalued downwards by $12,000 on 31 March 2017.
- The profit after tax for the year ended 31 March 2017 was $85,000.

a Prepare the journal entry (without narration) to record the **repurchase of shares** on 30 June 2016.

General Journal

b Prepare the **statement of changes in equity** for the year ended 31 March 2017.

Final Choice Limited
Statement of Changes in Equity for the year ended 31 March 2017

	Share capital	Retained earnings	Available-for-sale investments	Total equity
	$NZ	$NZ	$NZ	$NZ
Balance at 1 April 2016				
Changes in equity for 2017				

c Prepare the **ledger accounts** below for the year to 31 March 2017:

General Ledger

Share Capital

Retained Earnings

Fair Value Surplus

Available-for-sale Investments

Interim Dividend

Final Dividend

d Explain how the value of the available-for-sale investments would have been assessed at 31 March.

_____

_____

Andrew Scott and Bevan English are in partnership, trading as *Line Link Surveyors*. On 1 April 2014, the equity balances of the partners were as follows:

	Scott	English
Capital	$75,000 Cr	$50,000 Cr
Current	20,000 Cr	18,000 Cr
Drawings	45,000 Dr	35,000 Dr

The partnership has a five-year loan of $30,000 from Scott. This loan was made to the firm on 1 October 2014. The following information has been extracted from the partnership agreement:

- Interest on capital is payable at 8% per annum, based on the opening balance.
- No interest is to be paid on the first $10,000 of partners' current accounts. However interest of 10% per annum is payable on any part of the opening balance which exceeds this amount.
- Interest is charged on drawings at 5% per annum based on the average balance.
- Interest is payable on partners' loans at 12% per annum.
- Salaries are payable to partners as follows: Scott $50,000, English $40,000.
- Residual profits and losses are to be shared between the partners in the same ratio as their opening capital account balances.

The profit of the partnership, before interest on partners' loans, was $161,600 for the year ended 31 March 2015.

Prepare the **profit distribution** account for the partnership at 31 March 2015.

A Scott and B English *trading as* Line Link Surveyors
General Ledger

Profit Distribution

Date	Particulars	Debit	Credit	Balance
2015				
Mar 31	Profit and Loss		161,600	161,600 Cr
	Interest on drawings – Scott		1,125	162,725 Cr
	Interest on drawings – English		875	163,600 Cr
	Interest on loan – Scott	1,800		161,800 Cr
	Interest on capital – Scott	6,000		155,800 Cr
	Interest on capital – English	4,000		151,800 Cr
	Interest on current – Scott	1,000		150,800 Cr
	Interest on current – English	800		150,000 Cr
	Salary – Scott	50,000		100,000 Cr
	Salary – English	40,000		60,000 Cr
	Residual profit – Scott	36,000		24,000 Cr
	Residual profit – English	24,000		—

INDEX